THE CRITICAL ROLE OF FIRST RESPONDERS: SHARING LESSONS LEARNED FROM PAST ATTACKS

HEARING

BEFORE THE

COMMITTEE ON HOMELAND SECURITY
HOUSE OF REPRESENTATIVES

ONE HUNDRED THIRTEENTH CONGRESS

SECOND SESSION

JUNE 18, 2014

Serial No. 113–71

Printed for the use of the Committee on Homeland Security

Available via the World Wide Web: http://www.gpo.gov/fdsys/

U.S. GOVERNMENT PRINTING OFFICE

90–881 PDF   WASHINGTON : 2014

For sale by the Superintendent of Documents, U.S. Government Printing Office
Internet: bookstore.gpo.gov   Phone: toll free (866) 512–1800; DC area (202) 512–1800
Fax: (202) 512–2250   Mail: Stop SSOP, Washington, DC 20402–0001

CONTENTS

THE CRITICAL ROLE OF FIRST RESPONDERS: SHARING LESSONS LEARNED FROM PAST ATTACKS

Wednesday, June 18, 2014

U.S. House of Representatives,
Committee on Homeland Security,
Washington, DC.

The committee met, pursuant to call, at 10:05 a.m., in Room 311, Cannon House Office Building, Hon. Michael T. McCaul [Chairman of the committee] presiding.

Present: Representatives McCaul, King, Broun, Barletta, Hudson, Brooks, Sanford, Thompson, Jackson Lee, Clarke, Keating, Payne, and Vela.

Chairman MCCAUL. The Committee on Homeland Security will come to order. The committee is meeting today to examine testimony regarding the critical role first responders play in the protection of the homeland.

I now recognize myself for an opening statement.

The United States continues to face an ever-evolving terrorist threat from al-Qaeda, its affiliates, and others. We are seeing the rise of radical Islam in Africa, attacks by the Taliban in Pakistan and Afghanistan, and the civil war in Syria has provided a safe haven for terrorists to train, which is now flowing deep into Iraq. As I speak, a terrorist organization too extreme for al-Qaeda continues to march towards Baghdad leaving a trail of death, looting, and prison breaks.

These terrorists, and others around the world like AQAP, are intent on attacking the homeland. Just as we must continue to combat those threats overseas, we must also remain vigilant at home and be prepared to respond to attacks that reach our shores.

Today's hearing examines these terrorist events; first responder efforts before, during, and after these attacks; and the lessons learned.

Each day, first responders save lives and enhance the overall resiliency of our Nation. However, the 9/11 terrorist attacks forever changed the role of our emergency response providers. Since that day, these brave men and women have been the first on the scene during the 2009 shooting at Fort Hood and the 2013 Boston Marathon bombing, among others.

These tragic events remind us of the critical role first responders play in the Nation's ability to react quickly, whether it be to a terrorist attack or natural disaster. Lessons learned from previous ef-

(1)

forts are vital to increasing our ability to prepare for and respond to future incidents.

We owe it to these heroes and the American people to focus our efforts on doing all we can to ensure first responders are properly prepared for whatever catastrophe they encounter. From every incident, there are aspects of the response that went well and things that can be improved. We can and must learn from both.

This committee was formed in the aftermath of 9/11 to better protect the American people against a terrorist attack and fulfill its mission by ensuring that first responders, law enforcement personnel, and the Department of Homeland Security have the capabilities, training, and tools needed to prepare for, to prevent, and respond to future attacks.

In addition to the vital response and recovery mission, first responders are critical partners in preventing attacks. State and local law enforcement, fire, and emergency medical responders know their communities and will be the first to identify suspicious behavior and other potential security threats. First responders should have access to real-time threat and suspicious behavior reports, which are key to directing and detecting and stopping terrorism.

In turn, first responders must have access to all applicable Federal information so that they can do their job to the best of their ability. This was clear in the tragic Boston bombing last year.

Members of this committee are committed to seeing that the recommendations in the Boston Marathon bombing report are implemented, and most importantly, that information sharing between Federal, State, and local partners is improved.

I would like to recognize the first responders testifying here before us today, as well as those in the audience and across the country, for always answering the call. A simple "thank you" is not enough to express our gratitude for your efforts to protect the American people.

Thank you, and I look forward to your testimony.

With that, the Chairman now recognizes the Ranking Member.

Mr. THOMPSON. Thank you very much.

I want to thank the Chairman for holding today's hearing.

I also want to recognize the volunteers, first responders, and the citizens affected by the powerful tornadoes that ripped through the small town of Pilger, Nebraska. In a time of catastrophe, such as this, the first responder community runs to unsettled and unknown territory while others flee to safety.

I also thank the witnesses for their service and their dedication. Chief Schwartz, Deputy Commissioner Miller, and Chief Hooley are gentlemen who deserve commendation for their efforts.

I also thank Dr. Jackson for recognizing their efforts in his research.

Resilience and response are two of the reasons why almost a decade after September 11 New York City remains a global powerhouse. Resilience and response are two of the reasons why over 30,000 military and civilian personnel continue to serve at our Nation's defense headquarters in Arlington, Virginia. Resilience and response are two of the reasons why a year after the Boston Marathon bombing, Boston remains strong.

Mr. Chairman, as we rightfully commend today's panel, it would be a disservice to them not to address one of their main needs, which is funding.

In April this committee held a hearing on the Boston Marathon bombing. At that hearing Sergeant Pugliese, of the Watertown Police Department, testified that local municipal governments are not financially equipped to take on the increasing burden of catastrophic attacks, like Boston.

Last year at the Committee on Homeland Security's first hearing on the Boston Marathon bombing former Commissioner Davis stated that without grant funding the response would have been much less comprehensive than it was, and without the exercises supported through the Urban Area Security Initiative funding there would be more people who died in those attacks. Even today, Chief Schwartz is testifying that Federal grants serve as an incentive for bringing all agencies together before a terrorist event happens.

Throughout several Congresses, Members have heard about the importance of these grant programs and success stories involving them. Accordingly, I urge Members to oppose the administration's proposal to morph the Homeland Security Grant Program into an all-hazards grant. That proposal would shift focus away from supporting State and local efforts to develop terrorism-related prevention and preparedness capabilities.

I am not convinced that the administration's underfunded grant consolidation proposal would provide sufficient support for first responders across America to build and maintain the capabilities necessary to respond effectively. I cannot support any grant reform proposal until I am convinced that it would provide the support necessary to maintain terrorism preparedness capabilities we have spent over a decade building.

Also I agree with the Chairman that we cannot ignore the information sharing between Federal, State, and local authorities needs strengthening. Since September 11, information-sharing silos that the 9/11 commissioners recommended be addressed continue to be exposed after tragic events. We need to work together to develop ways to fix this problem post-haste.

Finally, Mr. Chairman, I ask that we continue this conversation with the Department of Homeland Security. We will hear about the challenges first responders have with working with both FEMA and the Office of Intelligence and Analysis, but we need to open hearings on what the Department is doing to address these matters. In that forum we may find ways that we can use our legislative platform to assist both DHS and the first-responder community.

With that, Mr. Chairman, I yield back the balance of my time.

[The statement of Ranking Member Thompson follows:]

STATEMENT OF RANKING MEMBER BENNIE G. THOMPSON

JUNE 18, 2014

I want to recognize the volunteers, first responders, and the citizens affected by the powerful tornadoes that ripped through the small town of Pliger, Nebraska. In a time of catastrophe such as this, the first responder community runs to unsettled and unknown territory while others flee to safety.

I also thank the witnesses for their service and dedication. Chief Schwartz, Deputy Commissioner Miller, and Chief Hooley are gentlemen who deserve commendation for their efforts. I also thank Dr. Jackson for recognizing their efforts in his research. Resilience and response are two of the reasons why almost a decade after September 11, New York City remains a global powerhouse. Resilience and response are two of the reasons why over 30,000 military and civilian personnel continue to serve at our Nation's defense headquarters in Arlington, Virginia. Resilience and response are two of the reasons why a year after the Boston Marathon bombings, Boston remains strong.

Mr. Chairman, as we rightfully commend today's panel, it would be a disservice to them not to address one of their main needs which is funding. In April, this committee held a hearing on the Boston Marathon bombing. At that hearing, Sergeant Pugliese of the Watertown Police testified that local municipal governments are not financially equipped to take on the increasing burden of catastrophic attacks like Boston.

Last year, at the Committee on Homeland Security's first hearing on the Boston Marathon bombings, former Commissioner Davis stated that without grant funding, the "response would have been much less comprehensive than it was" and without the exercises supported through Urban Area Security Initiative funding, "there would be more people who died in those attacks." And even today, Chief Schwartz is testifying that Federal grants serve as an incentive for bringing all agencies together before a terrorist event happens.

Throughout several Congresses, Members have heard about the importance of these grant programs and success stories involving them. Accordingly, I urge Members to oppose the administration's proposal to morph the Homeland Security Grant Program into an all-hazards grant. That proposal would shift focus away from supporting State and local efforts to develop terrorism-related prevention and preparedness capabilities. I am not convinced that the administration's underfunded grant consolidation proposal would provide sufficient support for first responders across America to build and maintain the capabilities necessary to respond effectively. I cannot support any grant reform proposal until I am convinced that it would provide the support necessary to maintain terrorism-preparedness capabilities we have spent over a decade building.

Also, I agree with the Chairman that we cannot ignore that information sharing between Federal, State, and local authorities needs strengthening. Since September 11, information-sharing silos that the 9/11 Commissioners recommended be addressed continue to be exposed after tragic events. We need to work together to develop ways to fix this problem post haste.

Finally, Mr. Chairman, I ask that we continue this conversation with the Department of Homeland Security. We will hear about the challenges first responders have with working with both FEMA and the Office of Intelligence and Analysis. But we need open hearings on what the Department is doing to address these matters. In that forum, we may find ways that we can use our legislative platform to assist both DHS and the first-responder community.

Chairman MCCAUL. I thank the Ranking Member.

Other Members are reminded they may submit opening statements for the record.

We are pleased to have a distinguished panel here before us today.

First, Deputy Commissioner John Miller. He is the deputy commissioner of intelligence for the New York City Police Department. Prior to this position, he was the senior correspondent for CBS News.

Commissioner Miller is also a former ABC News reporter, perhaps best known for conducting a May 1998 interview with Osama bin Laden. He is a former associate deputy director of national intelligence for analytical transformation and technology; and he was an assistant director of public affairs for the FBI, serving as the bureau's National spokesman.

Thank you, sir, for being here today.

Next we have Chief James Schwartz—if we could have some water? Chief James Schwartz is the chief of Arlington County Fire Department, a position he has held since 2004. The Arlington County Fire Department consists of 320 personnel and serves a community of 26 square miles and 210,000 residents. The department was the lead agency for the response to the September 11 attack at the Pentagon.

Additionally, Chief Schwartz chairs the International Association of Fire Chiefs' Committee on Terrorism and Homeland Security and served on the advisory council for the Interagency Threat Assessment Coordinating Group at the National Counterterrorism Center.

Thank you, sir, for being here today, as well.

Next we have Chief James Hooley, is the chief of the Boston Emergency Medical Services, a public safety agency that provides basic life support and advanced life support throughout the city of Boston. Boston EMS employs over 350 EMTs and paramedics who responded to an average of 300 emergencies per day.

A 32-year veteran of Boston EMS, he was appointed to the position in 2010. Prior to that he served as superintendent and chief.

What was left out of here I want to mention is the heroic efforts you and your force performed after the tragic events in Boston to save so many lives. With 260 maimed and injured, it is nothing short of a miracle that none of those maimed and injured actually died, and I want to thank you for those heroic efforts.

Finally, Dr. Brian Jackson is senior physical scientist at the RAND Corporation, director of RAND's safety and justice program, and a professor at Pardee RAND Graduate School. He focuses on homeland security, terrorism preparedness, safety management, and large-scale emergency response situations.

The full written statements of the witnesses will appear in the record.

Chairman now recognizes Commissioner Miller for 5 minutes.

STATEMENTS OF JOHN MILLER, DEPUTY COMMISSIONER, INTELLIGENCE AND COUNTERTERRORISM, NEW YORK CITY POLICE DEPARTMENT, NEW YORK, NEW YORK

Commissioner MILLER. Congressman McCaul, Congresswoman Clarke, Congressman King, Ranking Member Thompson, and Members of the committee, in the last 12½ years since September 11 the fight against al-Qaeda and its network has uncovered a very adaptable enemy that has continued to mature in its ability to spread its message as well as shift in its shape and its tactics. In response, the law enforcement community across the country has had to undergo fundamental changes.

In New York City, like every city and town, we have had to re-evaluate everything, from how we gather and analyze intelligence to how we plan to police major events. After 9/11 the New York City Police Department, under the leadership of Police Commissioner Ray Kelly, formed two new bureaus—the Intelligence Bureau and the Counterterrorism Bureau—to spearhead our efforts and Commissioner Bratton as well as Mayor de Blasio have made it clear that they would like to continue to build on, modernize, and sustain those efforts to protect the largest city in America from terrorist activity.

Today I want to spend a little time discussing lessons learned not just from 9/11 but also from other terrorist plots since then. Looking at some of the most recent and most significant, we take these lessons: We have learned that if al-Qaeda can find sympathizing people on U.S. soil that they will turn them into terrorists, willing and able to attack the very country they call home.

The cases of Najibullah Zazi, in the New York City subways plot in 2009, and Faisal Shahzad, the Times Square truck bomb plot in 2010, are just two examples of Americans, both recruited by al-Qaeda and the Pakistani Taliban, who attempted bombing of New York City. Law enforcement and intelligence was critical in thwarting those attacks.

We have also come to learn the power of al-Qaeda's use of social media and on-line messaging for operations and recruiting and communications. The Boston Marathon bombings, if anything, confirmed what we already always suspected, which is that major public events with large crowds are going to continue to be a terrorist target.

The instructions likely used by the Boston Marathon bombers to make pressure cooker bombs came from the now infamous article in al-Qaeda's on-line publication, *Inspire* magazine, "How to Make a Bomb in the Kitchen of Your Mom." Those same instructions were used by Jose Pimentel in New York City, who built bombs intending to blow up military and recruiting stations as well as other targets.

Recent issues of *Inspire* magazine call for al-Qaeda's followers to attack New York City as well as Washington, DC; Los Angeles; and Chicago. It is specific as to targets and timing.

The fact that we have seen people accept this call to arms reminds us that these threats can emanate from a camp hidden in the tribal areas of Pakistan or from an apartment in the Washington Heights section of Manhattan.

Counterterrorism is a major component of city planning and requires significant financial investments. Whether it is the Israeli Day Parade, which we had just a couple of weeks ago on 5th Avenue, or the New York City Marathon, each plan comes with a complex what we call "counterterrorism overlay."

Some of it you see, some of it is invisible, but all of it requires additional equipment, additional officers, intelligence analysts, detectives, and investigators. We deploy specialized equipment, from radiation detection pagers worn on people's belts to detect a dirty bomb or dispersal device attack, to a portable network of cameras to scan crowds.

To that end, I would like to thank this committee, the Congress, the President, the Department of Homeland Security for the continued critical support to New York City's Counterterrorism Grant funding. This funding has played a crucial role in helping the NYPD carry out its mission of keeping the city and its citizens safe.

The work and the equipment that goes with it, along with the personnel, is very expensive. The Counterterrorism Bureau receives money from eight funding streams, including UASI, for a total of $169.8 million. We have utilized these funds to deploy and develop adaptive approaches to countering threats, be they foreign or domestic.

Two major Federally-supported counterterrorism programs that I am talking about refer to:

The Domain Awareness System: It is an innovative law enforcement application that aggregates real-time data from counterterrorism sensors and law enforcement databases, providing members of the NYPD with a comprehensive view of potential threats as well as criminal activities.

The Securing the Cities Program: This is a program through which the NYPD purchases but also distributes radiation detection equipment to over 150 law enforcement and public safety agencies across the region, providing training, conducting exercises, and this develops a region-wide concept of operations for radiation detection.

These programs are critical to protecting New Yorkers, the region, and the Nation, and funding them remains an urgent priority.

Information sharing is also crucial to our efforts. Regional efforts in training and information sharing among law enforcement and first responders provide us with the necessary comprehensive response.

The NYPD is the lead agency for Securing the Cities Initiative, that interagency collaboration and capacity-building effort to protect the metropolitan region from nuclear or radiological attack. Examples of information sharing include interagency conference calls before major events; interagency meetings and tabletops with Federal, State, and local law enforcement agencies to discuss potential threats.

Public-private partnerships are also critical for first responders. The Lower Manhattan Security Initiative, or LMSI, is a public-private partnership that creates an information-sharing environment with the private sector, the NYPD, and other first responder agencies. This partnership leverages the security resources in place at some of the city's most high-profile target buildings and institutions, but it also forges partnerships that will facilitate an integrated response to incidents if there is an incident at any of these facilities or in that area.

The NYPD SHIELD program is a partnership with private-sector security managers with the goal of protecting the city from a terrorist attack. SHIELD includes members who work in a wide range of critical sectors, including the energy sector, and exchange information of concern as regards to terrorism and security.

On the Federal level, our Federal partners at DHS provide access to the Homeland Security Data Network, or HSDN, that enables information exchanges of both tactical and strategic intelligence and other homeland security information. The NYPD's partnership with the FBI also provides the NYPD with access to National Classified intelligence, but it is also a means by which the NYPD can disseminate its own intelligence and analysis at the Federal level to other Federal law enforcement agencies.

We continue to train in table-tops, live field exercises with multiple agencies to hone our response to the potential of another terrorist attack or active-shooter situation, or even natural disaster. With every drill, with every exercise, we glean lessons to better respond to real-world security threats.

The lessons learned post-9/11 focus on two key elements I have highlighted today. Resources: It takes additional resources—specialized equipment, training, and more money—to ensure police and first responders can effectively respond to events.

And coordination: We have learned again and again about the importance of sharing information and coordinating efforts. This is true on the Federal, State, and local level. We are safer and stronger when we work together as regions and coordinate across a range of first-responder entities.

The NYPD is a proud partner with the Federal Government in combating the threats to our National security. I thank you again, and especially this committee, for all your help to ensure the safety of the city of New York from these threats, and I pass along the thanks of our police commissioner, Bill Bratton, and Mayor de Blasio, in your support for those efforts.

[The prepared statement of Commissioner Miller follows:]

PREPARED STATEMENT OF JOHN MILLER

JUNE 18, 2014

Thank you Mr. Chairman and Members of the committee.

In the 12½ years since the horrific events of September 11, 2001, the fight against al-Qaeda and its network has uncovered an adaptable enemy that has continued to mature in its ability to spread its message as well as shift in shape and tactics. In response, the law enforcement community has undergone fundamental changes. In New York City, like every city and town, we have had to re-evaluate everything from how we gather and analyze intelligence, to how we plan for and police major public events. After 9/11, the New York City Police Department formed two new Bureaus, the Intelligence Bureau and the Counterterrorism Bureau, to spear-head our efforts to protect the Nation's largest city from terrorist activity.

Today, we examine the lessons learned not just from the 9/11 attacks, but also from the 16 other plots devised by al-Qaeda, or from those taking its cues, which have targeted New York City. Looking at some of the most recent and most significant, we take these lessons.

In 2009, Najibullah Zazi and three other men plotted to place more than a dozen backpacks filled with explosives on the New York subways. This plot was intended to kill scores of people and injure many more. Zazi traveled with his friends from Queens to Afghanistan in order to fight U.S. Forces, however, al-Qaeda recruited them to return to New York to launch these attacks once it was discovered that they were Americans, flying under the radar, with U.S. Passports that would easily allow them to return to the United States. Zazi was trained in explosives by none other than Rashid Rauch, who was al-Qaeda's top explosives expert at the time. Zazi also met with Saleh al-Somali, al-Qaeda's chief of external operations. From this case, we have learned that if al-Qaeda can find U.S. persons who are willing to fight and die in the fields of Afghanistan, they have a greater advantage in turning them back to launch attacks on the country they once called home.

This lesson was reinforced by the case of Faisal Shahzad. He traveled to Pakistan in an attempt to join fighters attacking U.S. forces in Afghanistan, but the Pakistani Taliban quickly identified him as an individual who could return to the United States and fight the war in our streets. Shahzad placed a large amount of explosives in an SUV in Times Square on May 1, 2010. However, a small technical error in his bomb-making saved our crowded Theater District in the streets off Times Square from destruction. We also learned from Shahzad that his pre-operational surveillance was conducted in a way that was unlikely to attract the attention of law enforcement. He chose his target by watching crowded conditions on different streets through streaming video over the internet from cameras in and around Times Square.

We have also come to learn the power of al-Qaeda's use of social media and on-line messaging to operatives that the terrorist leaders will never meet, or in some cases, may never even know are followers.

Jose Pimentel was a 27-year-old New Yorker who followed al-Qaeda's message through its on-line publication, *Inspire* magazine as well as the videos extolling violence by the charismatic al-Qaeda commander Anwar al-Awlaki. Al-Awlaki, born in New Mexico, spoke in perfect, unaccented English and his call to violence has resonated with a dozen plotters in the United States who have sought to kill their fellow Americans. Pimentel was arrested by NYPD Emergency Service Unit and Intelligence Bureau detectives while putting the final touches on a bomb he hoped to use to attack military recruiting stations.

Mohammed Quazi Nafis came to New York from Bangladesh and, inspired by al-Qaeda's magazine and al-Awlaki's videos, he set out to find partners to attack New York City's financial hub near Wall Street. He parked what he believed to be a thousand-pound bomb, hidden in the back of a white van, in front of the U.S. Federal Reserve and placed six calls from his cell phone to the number he thought was connected to the bomb's detonator. However, he had no idea that the bomb was designed by the FBI's New York Joint Terrorist Task Force not to function.

We learned from the Boston Marathon bombing what we already suspected; major public events, which attract large crowds, continue to be a terrorist target. The instructions likely used by the Boston bombers to make the pressure-cooker bomb came from the now infamous article, "How to Make a Bomb in the Kitchen of Your Mom," in *Inspire* magazine. Those same instructions were used by Jose Pimentel in New York City.

Recent issues of *Inspire* magazine feature stories idolizing the Marathon bombers as well as Jose Pimentel. The latest issue contains a set of instructions for a car bomb against a backdrop of pictures of Times Square. The article calls for those who believe in al-Qaeda's message to attack New York as well as Washington DC, Los Angeles, Chicago, and other major cities. The fact that we have seen people accept this call to arms, and to use the instructions that appear in *Inspire* magazine and similar publications, reminds us that the threat from al-Qaeda, whether through its central command, or its prolific propaganda machine, is still real. It can emanate from a camp hidden in the tribal areas of Pakistan or from an apartment in the Washington Heights section of Manhattan.

This is why it takes additional resources, specialized equipment, and more money to police events that used to simply require police personnel for crowd and traffic control. Whether it is the Israeli Day Parade, the Super Bowl Boulevard events in Times Square this past February, or the New York City Marathon, each plan comes with a complex counterterrorism overlay that requires additional equipment, officers, and investigators. We deploy specialized equipment from radiation detection pagers to detect a dispersal device attack to a portable network of cameras to scan the crowds. To that end, I would like to thank the committee, the Congress, and the Department of Homeland Security for the continued support to New York City's counterterrorism grant funding. This funding has played a crucial role in helping the NYPD carry out its mission of keeping the city and its citizens safe. It might be helpful to break that down:

The Counterterrorism Bureau receives money from 8 funding streams and 22 active grants, for a total of $169.8 million. These sources are:
- Urban Areas Security Initiative
- State Homeland Security Grant
- Law Enforcement Terrorism Prevention Program
- State Law Enforcement Terrorism Prevention Program
- Securing the Cities
- Transit Security Grant Program
- Port Security Grant Program
- National Nuclear Security Administration

Major Counterterrorism Bureau grant-funded projects include:
- *Domain Awareness System.*—An innovative law enforcement application that aggregates real-time data from counterterrorism sensors and law enforcement databases, providing members of the service with a comprehensive view of potential threats and criminal activity.
- *Securing the Cities Program.*—The NYPD purchases and distributes radiation detection equipment to over 150 law enforcement and public safety agencies across the region, provides training, conducts exercises, and develops a region-wide Concept of Operations for radiation detection.
- *Regional Counterterrorism Training*
- *World Trade Center Campus Security Plan and Environmental Impact Statement.*—A comprehensive vehicle security perimeter around the World Trade Center Campus, increasing stand-off distances from the buildings to reduce the risk of catastrophic damage from a vehicle-borne explosive device.
- *Explosive Detection Equipment Program*
- *Transit Security-Related Programs and Purchases*
- *Port Security-Related Programs and Purchases*

In addition to the grant funding, which is critical to our counterterrorism mission, information sharing is also crucial to our efforts. Examples of our information-sharing initiatives include:
- The Lower Manhattan Security Initiative is a public-private partnership that creates an information-sharing environment to leverage the security resources in place at some of the city's most targeted buildings and institutions and to

forge partnerships that will facilitate an integrated response to incidents at these facilities.

- The Joint Terrorism Task Force is a natural information-sharing environment between stakeholders including investigators, analysts, linguists, and other specialists from dozens of U.S. law enforcement and intelligence agencies.
- The NYPD's partnership with the FBI provides the NYPD with access to National Classified intelligence and is also a means by which the NYPD can disseminate its own intelligence and analysis at the Federal level and to other law enforcement agencies.
- A representative from the Metropolitan Transit Authority ("MTA"), New York State Courts, Federal Air Marshal Service, U.S. Marshal Service, and the Department of Homeland Security ("DHS") Federal Protective Services are detailed to the Counterterrorism Division and share information from their respective agencies.
- A Senior Intelligence Officer from the DHS Office of Intelligence and Analysis disseminates DHS-generated reporting, information from DHS Fusion Centers, and joint seal products like Joint Intelligence Bulletins.
- The NYPD is the lead agency for the Securing the Cities Initiative, an inter-agency collaboration and capacity-building effort to protect the metropolitan region from a nuclear or radiological attack. Examples of information sharing include inter-agency conference calls before major events like the Fourth of July and New Years Eve where Federal, State, and local law enforcement agencies discuss potential threats.
- NYPD SHIELD is a partnership with private-sector security managers with the goal of protecting NYC from terrorist attack. SHIELD includes members who work in a wide range of critical sectors, including the energy sector, and exchange information on issues of concern.
- DHS provides access to the Homeland Secure Data Network ("HSDN"). HSDN enables information exchange of both tactical and strategic intelligence and other homeland security information up to the SECRET level.
- Access to Suspicious Activity Reports.

Using Homeland Security funding and working with DHS partners in research and development, we have expanded our use of "Vapor Wake Dogs", the bomb detection K–9s that can identify if a suspicious package left unattended contains explosives, but can also detect the invisible vapor trail that indicates an explosive in a bag or a backpack is moving through a crowd on a busy street or public event. We have helped in the testing and development of virtual simulators that can put officers in "active-shooter" situations where they move down hallways and face the challenges of identifying shooters, rescuing hostages, or dealing with the wounded, while making critical tactical decisions. Controllers at the big screen see the same images being flashed through the officer's goggles to gauge and critique their tactical proficiency. We have applied Federal funding to the acquisition of highly-sensitive radiological detection equipment on-board our helicopters and harbor units that could detect a nuclear device aboard a cargo ship miles before it entered New York harbor. We continue to train, in table-tops and live field exercises with multiple agencies to hone our response to another terrorist attack, active-shooter situation, or natural disaster. With every drill, with every exercise, we glean lessons that will be invaluable if, or more likely when, we are faced with one of these real-world challenges in our streets.

I would be happy to answer any questions.

Chairman McCAUL. Please give him our thanks, as well.

Just for the record, the first city I visited was New York, recognizing it is still the biggest target, unfortunately.

Chairman now recognizes Chief Schwartz for—I am sorry, Chief—yes, Schwartz, for an opening statement.

STATEMENT OF JAMES H. SCHWARTZ, CHIEF, ARLINGTON COUNTY FIRE DEPARTMENT, ARLINGTON, VIRGINIA

Chief SCHWARTZ. Thank you, Chairman McCaul, Ranking Member Thompson, and distinguished Members of the committee. I want to thank you all for holding this hearing this morning as we look at lessons learned from past incidents of terrorism and devise strategies to better prepare our Nation for future events.

At 9:37 a.m. on September 11, 2001 American Airlines flight 77 crashed into the Pentagon as part of a large-scale attack upon the United States. I arrived on the incident scene at 9:48 and assumed incident command for the response.

There was an overwhelming response to the incident that included localities from the National Capital Region, the Commonwealth of Virginia, and multiple Federal agencies. This attack resulted in the deaths of 184 people.

Additionally, 106 patients received medical care by EMS and were transported to local hospitals, care centers, and clinics. Of those 106, only one person perished during treatment from her injuries received during the attack.

In the aftermath of that report the county undertook an after-action report that was eventually funded by the U.S. Department of Justice's Office for Domestic Preparedness. That report identified 235 recommendations and lessons learned that, along with other after-action reports in the last 13 years, have guided decisions that both the Arlington County public safety agencies and the National Capital Region have made to improve our preparedness levels.

On 9/11 it was extremely helpful that our fire department had a good working relationship—an amazing working relationship, I would say—with the FBI's Washington Field Office, the Military District of Washington, and other fire and rescue departments in the National Capital Region. These pre-existing working relationships at the incident command level and the existing automatic and mutual aid agreements throughout the region provided an experienced leadership team and necessary resources during the opening minutes of the response. In addition, we were able to use the incident command system to establish a unified command framework in which other resources and agencies could operate.

The after-action report also identified a number of challenges at the incident scene. Despite the coordination at the command level, we still had to contend with the challenges of self-dispatching and a lack of proper credentialing that—as we deployed our resources and strived to establish scene security.

One of our greatest challenges was in effectively triaging, treating, and tracking patients during this mass-casualty event. As has been well-documented, we had problems with operability and interoperability of our public safety communication systems, and logistics and resources for a long-term, large-scale incident proved at that time to be a challenge.

The Nation since then has transformed its emergency response system. The Federal Government has now established a National Preparedness Goal and 31 core capabilities to prevent, protect, mitigate, respond, and recover from a future incident. It also sponsored training exercises to improve preparedness and coordination at all levels of government. The Federal Government has also spent approximately $37 billion since 2002 on grant programs to support us at the State and local level in our preparedness efforts.

We have made important achievements to improve the coordination of response to future acts of terror. The adoption of the National Incident Management System allows jurisdictions across the Nation to work together during a response. That approach and a doctrinaire of using the same incident management system has assisted greatly in incidents since 9/11.

Multidisciplinary exercises bring together Federal, State, Tribal, territorial, and local agencies to plan and prepare for future events. The grants, such as those that we have already heard about from UASI and those from a previous program known as MMRS, have long served as incentives to bring stakeholders to the table to work on the common goals of preparing our communities.

Since 9/11, one major focus has been the improvement of public safety communications. This committee has taken a leading role in addressing this issue.

DHS and its Office of Emergency Communications, and Office of Interoperability Compatibility, and SAFECOM program are facilitating improved public safety communications interoperability. The President and Congress have played a major role in improving future public safety communications by establishing the First Responder Network Authority and giving it the adequate spectrum and funding to establish a Nation-wide public safety broadband network.

Even though there have been many accomplishments since 9/11, we are still learning to respond to the threat of terrorism. For example, there have been many initiatives to improve information-sharing between Federal, State, Tribal, and local partners.

However, there are still many barriers. The need for security clearances is still a barrier for many fire departments to obtain information about threats in their communities. In other cases, information may be over-Classified or not presented properly for practically-minded first-responder audience trying to develop capabilities necessary for response.

I want to commend the NCTC's approach to bringing first responders into the intelligence community to both share information from our perspective at the local level in the wake of the sunsetting of the ITACG, the Interagency Threat Assessment and Coordinating Group, the National Counterterrorism Center established the JCAT, the Joint Counterterrorism Assessment Team, that develops intelligence products with practical information for first responders and their communities.

We also must continue to focus on reducing barriers to collaboration. The NIMS adoption requires a change in culture for many organizations and we need to still bridge both the organizational and professional biases that are inherent in our organizations on a daily basis.

We should review NIMS training to ensure that all the participants in response to an incident are adopting NIMS and operating within it. Also, we have to support the current efforts to develop effective, Nation-wide credentialing system.

We also need to make sure that the lessons learned are being shared across the homeland security enterprise. The Pentagon response demonstrated that important and diligent planning and training at a regional-level paid dividends.

So that all stakeholders can learn from each other, we need to develop a clearinghouse for successful uses of grant programs and effective policies for countering threats to terrorism. In other words, when we have a success somewhere in the country, especially when it is a success realized through the grant programs, replicating that elsewhere is in everyone's best interest.

We also need to make sure that local first-responder agencies are being reimbursed for their mutual aid activities. In some cases it has taken years for local agencies to be reimbursed for their participation to responses like Hurricane Katrina and the October 2007 California wildfires.

In many jurisdictions budgets remain tight, and a local fire and EMS department cannot wait long to be reimbursed. The IAFC is concerned that local fire and EMS departments will not be as responsive in the future to requests for assistance if challenges to reimbursement remain a problem.

On behalf of the leadership of the Nation's fire and EMS service, I again want to thank you for the opportunity to testify today. Using the lessons of 9/11 and the accomplishments to date from those lessons learned has made the Nation, I think, stronger and has improved our overall preparedness.

However, the terrorist threat remains a continuing concern of all of ours and we must adapt to those concerns. I look forward to answering your questions as the committee hearing goes on.

Thank you.

[The prepared statement of Chief Schwartz follows:]

PREPARED STATEMENT OF JAMES H. SCHWARTZ

JUNE 18, 2014

Good morning, Chairman McCaul, Ranking Member Thompson, and distinguished Members of the committee. I am James Schwartz, chief of the Arlington County (Virginia) Fire Department (ACFD) and chairman of the Terrorism and Homeland Security Committee of the International Association of Fire Chiefs (IAFC). The IAFC represents the leadership of the Nation's fire, rescue, and emergency medical services (EMS), including rural volunteer fire departments, metropolitan career departments, and suburban combination departments. I thank the committee for this opportunity to discuss lessons learned from past incidents of terrorism.

THE RESPONSE TO THE INCIDENT AT THE PENTAGON ON SEPTEMBER 11, 2001

At 9:38 a.m. on September 11, 2001, American Airlines Flight No. 77 crashed into the Pentagon as part of a large-scale terrorist attack upon the United States. I arrived on scene at 9:48 a.m. and assumed incident command of the response. The main focus in the early hours of the response was to control the fires resulting from the crash and provide emergency medical care for the victims at the Pentagon. Sadly, the attack on the Pentagon claimed the lives of 184 people. Overall, the response to the Pentagon incident involved resources from across the National Capital Region (NCR), the commonwealth of Virginia, and multiple Federal agencies. The Arlington County Fire Department was the lead agency for unified command for 10 days and turned over primacy of command to the Federal Bureau of Investigation (FBI) on September 21.

In the early days of the response, Chief Ed Plaugher, my predecessor, instituted a process for collecting details of the response, so that they could be analyzed to create lessons learned. This analysis was produced as an after-action report by the Titan Systems Corporation that was funded with the support of the U.S. Department of Justice's Office for Domestic Preparedness. The report included 235 recommendations and lessons learned. In addition, the 9/11 Commission also reviewed the response to the attack on the Pentagon and made recommendations based on the analysis. The findings of these reports have been discussed in articles, conferences, and Congressional hearings over the past 13 years.

Despite the unfortunate loss of life, analysts have described the response to the Pentagon attack as being a successful one. During the response, 106 patients received medical treatment by area hospitals, care centers, and clinics. Of these 106 patients, only one person perished during treatment from her injuries.

During the Pentagon response, there were a number of factors that led to a successful response, mitigation, and recovery effort, and a number of challenges that the ACFD and other responding agencies faced. Among the factors that helped us were four major points:

(1) The ACFD had strong pre-existing relationships with surrounding jurisdictions and the affected Federal agencies.—Due to years of working together, the ACFD had strong support from the city of Alexandria; Fairfax, Prince William, and Loudoun county fire departments; the Metropolitan Washington Airports Authority; and other departments within the NCR. The FBI Washington Field Office established a fire liaison position in 1998 to work with local fire departments. The close working relationship between FBI Special Agent Chris Combs, a former New York firefighter, and the ACFD incident command staff played an especially beneficial role in ensuring a coordinated response.

Many of these relationships were developed through planning exercises. For example, the Military District of Washington hosts a major table-top exercise each year, which allows the leaders of Federal and local government organizations to learn to work together. In addition, Arlington County had conducted a May 2001 table-top exercise with military authorities about a scenario which featured a commuter airplane crashing into the Pentagon. This exercise helped the agencies to become familiar both with their own disaster plans and the plans of their military and civilian counterparts.

(2) Unified command through the Incident Command System ensured an effective response.—Within 3 minutes of the crash, then-Battalion Chief Bob Cornwell arrived on scene and established incident command. I arrived within 10 minutes of the crash and assumed incident command. Because the primary agencies responding to the incident all understood the Incident Command System (ICS), we were able to establish incident command within minutes and most of the other supporting agencies were able to operate within the framework. The fire departments in Northern Virginia began using ICS in the late 1980s and the Metropolitan Washington Council of Governments (COG) adopted the National Interagency Incident Management System (NIIMS) in March 2001, so that there already was a common command system in place. While the Military District of Washington has its own command structure, it cooperated with the ACFD as a member of unified command and provided necessary resources.

- *(3) A well-designed and exercised mutual aid system provided timely resources.*— At the time of the incident, and continuing today, Arlington County was a partner in the Northern Virginia Response Agreement wherein the jurisdictions provide automatic aid based on the closest fire and EMS unit, not jurisdictional boundaries. The departments operate under the same standard operating procedures and dispatch protocols. Also, there was a mutual aid agreement between the member governments of COG which was developed following the Air Florida crash in 1982. Finally, there was a State-wide mutual-aid agreement which enabled outlying jurisdictions to respond or to backfill for Alexandria and Fairfax County stations, while their units provided assistance to the ACFD.

- *(4) The Metropolitan Medical Response System laid the groundwork for successful coordination between emergency response and public health officials.*—After the 1995 sarin nerve agent incident in Tokyo, the ACFD realized that American first response agencies did not have the capability to respond to such an attack. At the request of Chief Plaugher and the ACFD leadership, the COG requested Federal assistance in building this capability. By working with the U.S. Public Health Service, the ACFD was able to develop the Nation's first locally-based terrorism response team with a hazardous materials, medical management, and mass-casualty decontamination capability, the Metropolitan Medical Strike Team (MMST). This capability became the Metropolitan Medical Response System (MMRS) and National Medical Response Team. The frequent use of exercises by the MMST and technical rescue teams provided for a coordinated response by the ACFD and surrounding jurisdictions. For example, the Arlington technical rescue team was able to integrate its personnel with the Alexandria team to form three teams of 19 persons each.

Despite the number of factors that led to a successful response, the ACFD also faced a number of challenges. The seven main challenges were:

- *(1) Self-dispatch created problems with the response.*—As news of the attack spread throughout the city, first responders from around the NCR arrived on scene to help with the response. These responders began aiding with the response without the request of the incident commander or knowledge of the host organization. In every major incident, self-dispatch is a problem. Unrequested volunteers are well-meaning, but they can complicate response operations by creating confusion at the incident scene. Also, if the incident commander is unaware of their actions, the self-dispatchers can put themselves at risk if they become injured or trapped. For long-term response and recovery operations, self-dispatched volunteers frequently do not come with the necessary food and shelter that they require, which creates an additional burden on the community trying to deal with the existing incident.

- *(2) Public safety communications were problematic during the Pentagon response.*—During the first hours of the response, cell phone networks were jammed, and cellular priority access service was not provided to emergency responders. Radio channels and phone lines to the emergency communications center also were jammed. In addition, there were problems with interoperability between jurisdictions. Pagers and runners proved to be the most effective form of communication. On September 12, the Incident Command Operations Section re-organized the fire suppression units into four divisions. This improved communications during the second day of operations.
- *(3) The Pentagon response identified room for improvement in the emergency medical response.*—During the response, triage tags were not used to document the care of victims. In addition, there was no system to document where patients were sent for treatment. The after-action report also identified the need for a clearinghouse hospital to coordinate communications on behalf of the medical community and disseminate patient disposition and treatment information.
- *(4) Logistics proved to be a challenge during the long-term incident response.*— Like many jurisdictions, the ACFD did not have the logistical infrastructure for dealing with an incident of the magnitude or duration of the Pentagon response. The stock of personal protective equipment (PPE), self-contained breathing apparatus (SCBA), batteries, medical supplies, and equipment for reserve vehicles were not sufficient for sustained operations. Fuel was a major requirement: In the first 24 hours, 600 gallons of diesel fuel were consumed. The resupply effort required 12 tractor-trailer loads for shoring operations, more than 5,000 pairs of gloves, thousands of Tyvek hazmat protection suits, and hundreds of respirators, SCBA, and air bottles. The Arlington County government, surrounding jurisdictions, like Fairfax County, and local business and relief organizations provided vital assistance in meeting this challenge.
- *(5) The need for credible situational information was a challenge during the incident.*—During the first 2 days of the response, it was important to get accurate situational information. The Pentagon incident scene had to be evacuated three times in the first 25 hours due to reports of incoming aircraft. These evacuations delayed some of the response operations and caused confusion at the incident scene.
- *(6) Resources also proved to be a challenge during the response.*—The after-action report identified the need for Arlington County to have a facility designed and equipped as an emergency operations center. It also recommended that the Arlington County Police Department upgrade its mobile command unit and that the fire department obtain a mobile command vehicle for on-scene incident management. The report identified improvements that needed to be completed in the emergency communications center to enhance communications and operations during another major incident. In addition, ACFD and other departments did not have access to a deployable supply of mass casualty supplies, which meant that medical supplies had to be taken from EMS units.
- *(7) The Pentagon response demonstrated the need for a credentialing system for first responders.*—During the response and recovery effort, it was important to make sure that authorized first responders had access to the incident scene. Unfortunately, there was no credentialing system to identify personnel and their skills. The DHS has worked on a number of reports and pilot projects over the years to address this system, but it currently remains unresolved. A First Responder Access Card was pilot-tested, but it proved to be too expensive and too hard for jurisdictions to maintain the database. The DHS' Office of Infrastructure Protection has developed a new system with State and local first responders, which has been adopted by four States. Another six States are in the process of adopting it.

APPLICATION OF LESSONS LEARNED

The Nation has transformed its emergency response system since the attack on the Pentagon. The Final Report of the National Commission on Terrorist Attacks Upon the United States (also known as the 9/11 Commission Report) described the events leading up to the 9/11 attacks, the attacks themselves, and the response. In addition, it made a number of recommendations, many of which Congress has implemented through legislation. Overall, Federal, State, and local agencies; the private sector; and members of the American public have made many changes over the years based on the responses to 9/11 to better prepare the Nation for future terrorist threats.

The Federal Government has become an important partner in the effort to prepare for the next terrorist attack. It has established a National Preparedness Goal and 31 core capabilities to help the Nation to prevent, protect, mitigate, respond to, and recover from an incident, whether from natural or human cause. In addition, the Federal Government has sponsored training to respond to terrorist attacks, and exercises at the Federal, State, Tribal, territorial, and local level. The Federal Government also has spent approximately $37 billion since 2002 on grant programs to help State and local agencies develop the training, equipment, and staffing resources required to meet the terrorist threat.

One important development is the adoption of the National Incident Management System (NIMS). The NIMS is the comprehensive, Nation-wide approach to incident management. Based on the ICS that the fire and emergency service uses, it allows jurisdictions around the country to work together in response to an emergency. Much as fire departments were able to coordinate and respond together during the 9/11 response to the Pentagon, response agencies from around the Nation will be able to work together to respond to future all-hazards events using NIMS. NIMS is scalable and can be used for any National incident, no matter the size or duration. The NIMS system is focused on defining core terminology and defining resources, so that a fire chief can request an asset from anywhere in the United States and have a reasonable expectation of what is being received. Federal grant programs provide assistance in NIMS adoption, because a grantee must comply with NIMS in order to receive grants from the Federal Emergency Management Agency (FEMA).

In addition, there is an improved focus on mutual aid and collaboration. Mutual aid from surrounding departments played a major role in the response to the Pentagon attack. There is a greater emphasis now on multidisciplinary exercises that bring Federal, State, Tribal, territorial, and local agencies together to build partnerships and prepare for future threats. One of the most important lessons from the Pentagon response is that it is important for the leaders and staff of Federal, State, Tribal, territorial, and local agencies to work and plan before any incident occurs. These existing relationships will create an effective response when it is needed. It is important to highlight the role that Federal grant programs, such as the Urban Areas Security Initiative (UASI) and MMRS, serve as incentives for bringing all of the agencies together before a terrorist attack happens.

One primary focus since the Pentagon incident is the need to improve communications interoperability. DHS offices, including the Office of Emergency Communications and the Office for Interoperability and Compatibility, have played an important role in facilitating improved communications between State and local public safety agencies. SAFECOM is a Federal effort, led by local first responders, to improve multi-jurisdictional and intergovernmental communications interoperability. It trains emergency responders to be communications unit leaders during all-hazards emergency operations, and coordinates grant guidance to use Federal funding to encourage interoperability. SAFECOM focuses both on technology and the need for jurisdictions to develop an effective command interoperability plan. President Obama and Congress also made an important decision to improve future public safety communications by setting aside 20 MHz for a dedicated Nation-wide public safety broadband network and establishing the First Responder Network Authority (FirstNet) to govern it as part of the Middle Class Tax Relief and Job Creation Act of 2012 (Pub. L. No. 112–96).[1]

There also is an increased focus on improving information sharing between Federal, State, and local response agencies. The Federal Government has helped to fund 78 fusion centers around the Nation that serve as focal points for receiving, analyzing, and sharing threat-related information between Federal, State, local, Tribal, and territorial partners. In addition, programs like the Nation-wide Suspicious Activity Reporting Initiative and "See Something, Say Something" campaign allow first responders to report possible threats in their jurisdictions.

At the local level, jurisdictions around the NCR implemented changes to improve their response to future terrorist attacks. Funding by the UASI program allowed the NCR agencies to develop standardized regional capabilities, including mass casualty units and ambulance buses; bomb teams; and air units to refill firefighters' SCBAs during an incident. The NCR jurisdictions also used UASI funds to interconnect the

---

[1] It is important to note that FirstNet will originally cover only broadband data communications, such as streaming video. Local first responders will need to continue to rely upon land-mobile radio for mission-critical voice communications for at least the next 10 years.

local fiber optic networks into one "NCR Net." This system uses the seamless transition of critical data, including computer-aided dispatch systems, throughout the region to improve situational awareness and reduce emergency call processing time.

CHALLENGES FOR THE FUTURE

It is important to recognize that, even though the attack on the Pentagon took place 13 years ago, we are still learning to respond to the threat of terrorism. New threats continuously appear and we must adapt to them. For example, while we still must prepare for an explosive attack on a major transportation hub or an act of bio-terrorism, we also have to prepare for the use of fire as a weapon in a terrorist attack or an active-shooter assault by a small team as happened in Mumbai in 2008 and Nairobi in 2013.

In recognition of this fact, I would like to raise the following issues for the committee's jurisdiction:

- *(1) We need to continue to focus on NIMS adoption.*—One of the keys to any successful response is the ability for various units to communicate and operate together. The adoption of NIMS requires a culture change, and we still need to bridge organizational and professional biases. We need to review NIMS training and ensure that Federal, State, local, Tribal, and territorial partners are all adopting NIMS and operating with it.
- *(2) We need to make sure that lessons learned are being shared to improve the homeland security enterprise.*—We need to better broadcast successful uses of grant programs and encourage the adoption of successful policies. For example, the NCR developed a patient tracking system to track victims' basic information and conditions, which allows them to be distributed to hospitals and tracked throughout their time in the system. If another jurisdiction is interested in developing a similar system, it should be able to find out about it at a clearing-house instead of having to re-invent the wheel.

  In addition, we should support the development of regional response systems. The Pentagon response relied upon resources throughout the Washington and Northern Virginia areas. This coordination was established years before through the activities of the COG. One of the IAFC's concerns with the National Preparedness Grant Program proposal is its State-centric focus, which we think might break down the sort of regional coordination required to effectively respond to cross-border incidents.
- *(3) We need to improve information sharing both about the potential for terrorist activity and during an incident.*—The attacks on 9/11 exposed a host of information-sharing problems at the Federal, State, Tribal, territorial, and local level, both before and during the incident. During the Pentagon response, the incident scene had to be evacuated three times, due to the perceived threat of another incoming airplane. At least two of these incidents were caused by Federal officials arriving in Washington to help with the Federal response to these attacks. The Federal Government needs to make sure that accurate information is being relayed to the first responders on scene so that they can make the appropriate decisions.

  In addition, problems still remain with the information-sharing enterprise. The need for a security clearance remains a barrier for some fire chiefs to access information. However, once a chief receives information, he or she is limited with what can be done with it, because command staff may not have clearances. In other cases, information may be over-Classified or not written with a practical purpose. The National Counterterrorism Center's (NCTC) Joint Counterterrorism Assessment Team helps to solve this problem by bringing local first responders to the NCTC to work with intelligence analysts to develop intelligence products with practical information that first responders can use to protect their communities. To help fire chiefs better understand how to access threat information for their communities, the IAFC developed the Homeland Security Intelligence Guide for Fire Chiefs.
- *(4) We need to ensure that local first-response agencies are being reimbursed for their mutual aid activities.*—The National Preparedness Goal aims to create a National network of resources and capabilities. However, it is important to recognize that State and local governments spend approximately $218 billion annually for public safety. When a resource is dispatched from a locality across local or State lines to help with a mutual aid response, the local first response agency potentially can lose those resources for weeks and will have to backfill to protect its community. For major emergencies, such as Hurricane Katrina and the October 2007 California wildland fires, a local fire department can be left waiting for months or even years to get reimbursed. In many jurisdictions,

budgets remain tight and a local fire and EMS department cannot wait that long to be reimbursed. The IAFC is concerned that fire and emergency departments will not be as responsive to future requests for assistance during major National emergencies if the reimbursement system is not reformed and improved.

CONCLUSION

I would like to thank the committee for the opportunity to discuss the response to the Pentagon attack on 9/11 and the lessons learned from it. The events of 9/11 were a terrible tragedy. The Nation has made many improvements to its National preparedness system to prevent such a tragedy from happening again. However, the terrorist threat continues to adapt, and we must adapt to meet it. Both the IAFC and I look forward to working with the committee to face these new challenges and protect our communities.

Chairman McCAUL. Thank you, Chief Schwartz.
Chairman recognizes Chief Hooley.

STATEMENT OF JAMES HOOLEY, CHIEF, BOSTON EMERGENCY MEDICAL SERVICES

Chief HOOLEY. Morning. Chairman McCaul, Ranking Member Thompson, and Members of the committee and staff, I want to thank you for your invitation to testify today on the critical role of first responders and sharing lessons learned from past attacks.

My name is James Hooley. I serve as the chief of department at Boston EMS.

Boston EMS is responsible for the provision of emergency medical services for the city of Boston. We are best described as a municipal third service EMS system, in that we are part of the city's health department and are separate from fire or police, who we do work closely with.

I wish to thank the mayor of Boston, Martin J. Walsh, and the executive director of the Boston Public Health Commission, Dr. Barbara Ferrer, for their support of my participation here today.

I also want to acknowledge the dedicated EMTs and paramedics from across our country, and in particular, the men and women of Boston EMS who distinguished themselves on April 15, 2013 and play a critical role in ensuring the safety and health of Boston every day.

On Patriots' Day—Monday, April 15, 2013—two IEDs were detonated 10 seconds apart on the sidewalk of Boylston Street in Boston. The sites were crowded with spectators watching the Boston Marathon.

In an instant a large sporting event and day of civic pride was transformed into a mass casualty incident. Three persons were killed immediately while 118 survivors would require transport by ambulance due to the nature of their injuries.

Within minutes, 30 patients were categorized as critical, 25 as serious, and the remainder with non-life-threatening injuries. Those critical and serious patients were rapidly identified, given life-saving treatment, quickly transported to hospitals. The patients with lower-acuity injuries were transported next. The scene was cleared within 22 minutes and the last of the non-acute patients was transported within the hour.

Boston's hospitals enacted their mass casualty operations plans to effectively care for this surge of patients. In the hours that followed, approximately 260 patients would seek medical treatment.

We acknowledge the loss—excuse me—while acknowledging the loss, the pain, and the suffering still felt today by survivors and their loved ones, I can say that the medical response to this attack was a success. It was successful because of a system that was built in Boston which put us in the best posture to succeed.

A lot of things went right. There was extensive pre-event planning by public safety, hospital, and public health agencies. Those plans were tested in drills and table-top exercises. Staging and loading areas had been pre-determined.

A large contingent of EMS and other first responders—medical volunteers—were prepositioned for the response, and they did not hesitate to render aid and assist with the extrication of patients despite the risk of other bombs.

Interoperability worked. We were able to immediately communicate with all the emergency rooms in the city at once. We could immediately communicate with several ambulance services simultaneously.

Boston EMS coordinated the triage care and rapid transport of 118 individual patients and we distributed them across 9 area hospitals. Patients were triaged, provided essential life-saving treatment such as tourniquets, and transport was expedited.

Boston CMED assigned ambulances to hospitals based on their capacity and capability. Boston has five Level-1 adult trauma centers as well as a Level-1 trauma center that is specific for pediatrics.

Private citizens stepped up and became first responders that day. Information sharing was supported by us having a medical intelligence center, which was activated.

There were some issues that did not go as well. In the immediate aftermath there was some apprehension and confusion as reports of possible other attacks in the city had to be investigated. In transporting that many acute patients so quickly, many of whom—who had altered mental status or missing personal effects, that delayed patient identification.

In some cases, the rules of privacy and restrictions on sharing patient information resulted in delays in reuniting patients with their loved ones. This did not impact the survivors' care, but the frustration felt by their families added to their stress.

Fortunately, most things did go right that day, but we were left to wonder the "what-ifs." What if the attack had occurred somewhere else, at a different time of day, or if other complicating factors had been present?

There are valuable lessons learned that I can share.

Ambulance surge capacity is vital. As I pointed out, half the patients required immediate transport. Having sufficient ambulances available was life-saving.

Planning works. The Boston Regional Mass Casualty Plan ensures that assisting agencies will have the same language, procedures, and equipment. Having sound operational plans with realistic assumptions makes those plans adaptable.

Be prepared. Never assume that an attack, accident, or natural disaster won't happen in your city. In fact, assume that it will.

Training works. Over the years we took part in many WMD trainings and drills, mass-casualty drills, including training with the Boston Police Department to provide EMS in high-turn environments, such as bombings or in mass shootings. So when the real event did occur, our personnel were rehearsed.

EMS can operate in unsecured scenes. As in our case, EMTs with PPE and trained to understand the risks and taking precaution can quickly operate and maximize patient survival while under the protection of law enforcement.

Plan for bystanders to respond. Dozens of bystanders stepped in to help that day. Many of them had medical training or prior military experience and they were invaluable. We need to be able to quickly identify those force multipliers at future events.

In the days and weeks that followed, we worked hard to capture the lessons learned. Boston EMS solicited input from our members, including a series of after-action meetings that we held, and also we had one-on-one interviews.

We also hosted sessions with our private ambulance partners who assisted us. We attended the after-action reviews at Boston hospitals to share best practices and what will improve future events.

We are incorporating these lessons learned into planning for future events, and many have already been put into operation.

I believe that the Federal Government was very helpful in preparing us for the series of events that occurred that week in Boston. In the past, Boston has benefitted from State Homeland Security grant and MMRS programs.

In recent years the UASI program has proven to be very beneficial at providing training, exercises, PPE, and equipment. In Boston the Mayor's Office of Emergency Management effectively administers this grant. Investment areas that support multiple jurisdictions and disciplines in all hazards are the ones more likely to be approved.

EMS, hospitals, and public health have had significant input in the Boston UASI program, and as a result we were all better prepared.

I would ask Congress to continue their support to the UASI program, as it has proven value. I would also recommend that communities across the country that receive Homeland Security grants include EMS, hospitals, and public health, as their roles and needs must be represented.

EMS and health care should also have inclusion within fusion centers. Boston EMS has been fortunate to assign one of our members to the Boston Regional Intelligence Center since 2007, and that has served us well.

Thank you all for the opportunity to address you today, and thank you for your on-going efforts in protecting our homeland.

[The prepared statement of Mr. Hooley follows:]

PREPARED STATEMENT OF JAMES HOOLEY

JUNE 18, 2014

BOSTON EMERGENCY MEDICAL SERVICES

Boston EMS is the lead agency for the provision of emergency medical services within the city of Boston, Massachusetts and a bureau of the Boston Public Health Commission. As a municipal public safety department, Boston EMS is separate from both the Police and Fire Departments, but an active partner in the provision of

9–1–1 emergency services. In 2013, Boston EMS processed 116,637 9–1–1 emergency medical incidents, resulting in 142,341 ambulance responses and 83,144 patient transports to hospital emergency departments. The service is comprised of 375 full-time positions, including EMTs and paramedics, as well as uniformed supervisors and command staff, certified mechanics, support and administrative personnel. In addition to the 24 front-line ambulances staffed during peak day and evening shifts, Boston EMS is responsible for the city's medical 9–1–1 dispatch center, which supports call-taking, dispatching, and managing the region's Central Medical Emergency Dispatch (CMED) communication between EMS personnel and receiving hospitals.

BOSTON MARATHON AND THE BOMBINGS

The marathon is one of Boston's largest annual special events, although less than 3 miles of the actual course are within the city itself. In 2013, there were approximately 27,000 registered runners, 8,000 volunteers, and hundreds of thousands of observers lining the streets along the route. With the finish line in the heart of Boston, most medical assets, including both Boston EMS personnel and Boston Athletic Association volunteers, were concentrated in this area.

At 2:49 p.m. the first explosion occurred by the finish line, at Copley Square. Ten seconds later the second bomb was detonated. Boston EMS personnel assigned to the zone by the finish area were able to immediately confirm there had been explosions. This was followed by a notification over the radio that "two devices went off". All units were notified to take extreme caution. Personnel at Alpha Medical Tent were told to prepare to receive patients and hospitals were notified via a disaster radio that there had been a mass casualty event. Private ambulance mutual aid was requested at 2:55 p.m. via the Boston Area Mutual Aid network (BAMA) and the first patient was transported at 2:58 p.m. A total of 118 individuals were transported by ambulance in the aftermath of the bombings. Within minutes, 30 patients were categorized as critical, 25 as serious and the remainder with non-life threating injuries. Those critical and serious patients were rapidly identified, given life-saving treatment and quickly transported to hospitals. The patients with lower acuity injures were transported next. The scenes were cleared in 22 minutes and the last of the non-acute patients was transported within the hour. Boston's hospitals enacted their mass casualty operations plans to effectively care for this surge of patients. In the hours and days that followed, approximately 260 patients would seek medical treatment.

WHAT WENT RIGHT

While acknowledging the loss, pain, and suffering still felt today by survivors and their loved ones, the medical response to the attack was a success, serving as a testament to the level of preparedness, planning, and training our city and State have achieved. Everyone who left the scene alive is still alive today, a remarkable outcome given the severity and number injured.

In exploring what went right, it is imperative to first address the circumstantial elements that worked in our favor, such as: (1) The proximity of the bombs to ready medical assets, (2) the availability of qualified personnel to commence rapid and appropriate triage, treatment, and transport, (3) the optimal running conditions, resulting in reduced marathon-related illnesses and injuries, allowing resources to be appropriately redirected to those injured by the two bombs, (4) the incidents occurred immediately before hospital shift change, resulting in added staffing in the midst of the patient surge. It is also important to note that Boston has 6 level-1 trauma centers, one of which exclusively serves pediatric patients (Boston Children's Hospital), allowing the most critical patients to promptly receive the care they needed. By acknowledging the elements that worked in our favor, we recognize the possibility that maybe next time they won't (for us or another city), and we plan for it.

Focusing on the elements of the response where we did have influence, it is important to highlight the years of behind the scenes planning, coordinating, drilling, exercising and training that allowed us to have the best possible outcome, given the circumstance.

Homeland Security Grants

From the time Homeland Security grants first became available to us, both the State and city have worked actively to make the most of the opportunities they have afforded. We are grateful for the years of State Homeland Security Program and Urban Areas Security Initiative funding. Many of the investments we have made with these dollars served a direct benefit in response to the bombings, including trainings, exercises, equipment, and PPE.

Emergency management and homeland security grant investments in the region have a long-standing history of being inclusive of not only EMS, but also non-public safety partners, such as hospitals, health centers, long-term care centers, and businesses. With most training, drills and exercises being both inter-jurisdictional and inter-disciplinary, the response to the bombings was inevitably inclusive and coordinated. Personnel utilized shared protocols, shared ICS language, and understood what and how they needed to communicate to others and what they could depend on them for.

Joint Training and Exercises

The joint trainings and exercises have been invaluable, not just for the experience of the participants, but also the many months of planning that bring agencies across disciplines together. Even departments that respond jointly on a routine basis, benefit from shared trainings and exercises to prepare for the less routine. As an example, Boston EMS trains extensively with the Boston Police Department SWAT and Bomb Squad units, so that our EMTs and Paramedics are appropriately integrated into their responses.

Learning From Others

Just as others listen and learn from our experiences, we have spent the last 2 decades, doing the same with other communities across the country and the world. Whether it was the terrorist attacks in London, Oklahoma, Madrid, New York, Mumbai, or Columbine; or the natural disasters that swept through New Orleans, the Texas coast, and New Jersey, we critically examined what we would have done if the same were to happen in Boston. We tried to incorporate the successes we saw the other first responders implement and did our best to apply their lessons learned.

Extensive Inter-Agency Pre-Event Planning

Meetings to prepare for the race commence a year prior, with an extensive array of stakeholders, including emergency management, public health, EMS, hospitals, police, and the American Red Cross. Prior to the race, the Massachusetts Emergency Management Agency hosts a table-top exercise focused on a particular disaster scenario/race disruption. Through years of exploring what could go wrong, much was done to prepare, including pre-identified shelters, staging locations and loading areas, in addition to pre-positioned mass casualty supplies. Many of the existing plans for the marathon, such as taking all critical patients to the back of Alpha Medical Tent, where Boston EMS had a designated treatment and ambulance loading area, worked well in response to the bombings.

Special Events As Planned Disasters

Over the years, Boston saw the potential for large-scale special events, such as the Boston Marathon, to not only be locations of heightened risk for attacks, due to their high-profile nature and large crowds, but also serve as opportunities to implement, test, and gain familiarity with NIMS and ICS practices. In fact, we began referring to special events as "planned disasters", given that they inherently share many of the same characteristics. Between 1- and 2,000 runners seek medical care at a course medical station and/or hospital during the Boston Marathon, many partner agencies are involved, streets are congested, and access can be compromised. Incorporation of the National Incident Management System and the Incident Command System, as well as utilizing equipment, resources, and systems designed for large-scale emergencies helps with the overall medical consequences of the event. And, the experience provides personnel an opportunity to gain familiarity with disaster response protocols, a practice that also allows for a seamless transition if/when a real emergency arises, whether it is an evacuation at the Boston Pops Fourth of July celebration, due to a thunderstorm, or terrorist attacks at the Boston Marathon.

There Were Ready Medical Assets That Did Not Hesitate to Render Aid

Understanding both the potential for a significant volume of marathon-related illnesses and injuries, as well as the risk for something worse, Boston EMS personnel, other first responders and medical volunteers were heavily concentrated near the finish area. We had nearly a third of our workforce, a total of 116 EMTs and paramedics, assigned to Zone 1, the finish area. An additional 13 ambulances, and associated personnel, were staged at the event and 26 were working city-side, two above the normal day-shift complement. When the bombs exploded there was an immediate shift to mass casualty mode. A second device had already detonated and there was a possibility of more, yet, there was no hesitation in going directly to the blast sites and expediting extraction, care, and transport.

Boston EMS coordinated the care and rapid transport of 118 individual patients, distributing them across 9 area hospitals. Patients were triaged, provided essential life-saving treatment, such as tourniquets, and transport was expedited. Boston CMED then assigned ambulances to hospitals based on their capacity and capability.

Interoperability Worked

When the request was sent for ambulance mutual aid support, the response was immediate. With years of coordination and shared training, they reported directly to the designated staging area, allowing for fluid loading and transport, with the most critical being transported first. Similarly, Boston EMS was able to communicated via disaster radios to all emergency departments in the city at once, as planned. When they received the notification they understood the implications and took necessary actions to prepare.

Patient Distribution

The survival of a patient in critical condition is dependent upon receiving appropriate care, making not just rapid transport, but also the availability and capability of the hospital, essential. Many post-disaster best practices have emerged over the years, cautioning the tendency to transport to the closest hospital. Taking note, we have spent years coordinating with our EMS and hospital partners to plan for patient distribution during a multi-casualty incident. At the end of the day, no one hospital was overwhelmed by the volume of patients they received, in response to the bombs; we consider this to be the best measure of successful patient distribution.

WHAT WENT WRONG

Aside from the most egregious wrong, the fact that Boston experienced a terrorist attack, three lost their lives, 16 suffered amputations and many more were injured; Boston has spent many months evaluating how we could have done a better job.

In the immediate aftermath, there was some apprehension, confusion, and reports of other possible attacks. Transporting such a high volume of acute patients so quickly, with many unresponsive or missing identification, coupled with privacy rule restrictions on sharing information, resulted in delays for identifying some patients and reuniting them with loved ones. It did not affect the survivors' care, but the frustration experienced by their families was real.

Fortunately, most went right and we were left to wonder the "what ifs": Had the attacks occurred elsewhere, at a different time of day or if other complicating factors had been present. People speak of the Boston Standard, but ultimately, the challenge is on us to ensure we can meet that standard in other scenarios.

LESSONS LEARNED

EMS Surge Capacity is Vital to Patient Survival During an MCI

The experiences of April 15, 2013 and the week that followed highlighted both strengths and areas for improvement in our public safety response capabilities. Speaking from the emergency medical services perspective, our greatest success also points to one of our most significant challenges. Having experienced and trained professionals on scene, able to provide immediate treatment and transport saved lives, but this EMS surge capacity was in many respects artificial; it is not part of daily operations.

EMS has a public safety role that complements the Fire and Police functions. Regardless whether EMS is embedded within another organization, a private agency or a municipal third service, we as a country must critically examine its ability surge. As we push health-care functions to become less costly and more efficient, reducing periods of ambulances not being assigned to calls to as close to zero as possible, we expose ourselves to a point of self-organized criticality, where we can't respond to the "what-if" scenarios. We are grateful to our private ambulance mutual aid partners, who answered the call when we requested their assistance on April 15, but it is uncertain where ambulances would come from should an incident happen on a different day of the year. Fiscal realities affect municipal as well as private ambulance capacity and staffing.

Chance Favors the Prepared

Louis Pasteur once said, "chance favors the prepared mind," a phrase that is well-suited for the field of homeland security. Having frequently employed NIMS and ICS protocols in real incident and special event response efforts, their use was natural and automatic after the explosions. For years, we would imagine the unimaginable and then take action to expand our knowledge and capabilities in that area.

We have hosted conferences on various potential threats, including improvised explosive devices, invested in medical supplies for trauma care, spent years training and drilling our personnel on triage and mass casualty incident response, and participated in multiple full-scale exercises, a number of which included blast incident scenarios and lent experience to skills in interagency coordination and patient distribution.

Initially focused on supporting the added logistical challenges associated with the central artery tunnel project, known as the Big Dig, the Boston EMS Special Operations Division, has evolved into an essential element of preparedness within the Department and the city. The division coordinates medical consequence resources for over 500 special events each year, as well as providing logistical support for unplanned emergencies. Having such an integral component of the Department dedicated to planning for the expected and unexpected, fosters a Department-wide culture of preparedness.

Training and Exercises Work

Department of Homeland Security grant funding has been invaluable in supporting inter-disciplinary inter-jurisdictional training and exercises. The integration of public safety agencies from multiple cities and towns, as well as non-public safety partners, including hospitals and public health, has not just increased individual staff knowledge, but has also helped agencies understand how to respond together in a collaborative manner, respecting each other's roles and strengths. The more we are able to provide opportunities for personnel to train and exercise together, the more it becomes second nature. We are appreciative of a supportive Office of Emergency management, which has prioritized such opportunities, and for FEMA for approving them.

The more responders understand the protocols and priorities of other disciplines, the more they are able to work collaboratively, in support of a shared success. International Trauma Life Support standards promote principals in trauma care for EMS that mirror combat care in the military, focusing on rapid assessment, treatment, and transport; if public safety partner agencies understand this, they may better recognize how they can support this function, such as securing routes for ambulance ingress and egress from an incident to maximize patient survival.

In addition to local trainings, I can personally attest to the benefit of programs focused on strategic leadership, such as the Naval Post Graduate School, Center for Homeland Defense and Security, where I joined a cohort of local, State, and Federal representatives, from both public and private sectors. This executive-level program provided an invaluable opportunity to more critically examine issues in homeland security and share lessons learned with other public safety and emergency management leaders. This program serves as a reminder of how important it is to be continually learning, particularly when we work in a field where we are expected to protect the public from ever-evolving threats.

Planning Works

In Boston, EMS, hospitals, and public health are well integrated into planning teams. Having diverse representation for this component helps mitigate false assumptions about a discipline's capabilities and serves as an opportunity to communicate priorities that may not be readily apparent to others. By seeking value in such partners, emergency management has benefited from a broader platform of subject-matter experts and built a more cohesive and prepared community.

As a coordinated effort with our private EMS partners, Boston has a regional MCI plan. And, all large-scale special events, such as the Boston Marathon have a medical consequence plan that is updated and reviewed each year. Such plans are successful because they are well-practiced and adaptable. We can write planning documents, train, exercise, and invest in equipment, but ultimately, we have to trust in our personnel to improvise, adapt, and overcome. If they can understand the end-goal of what they are being asked to do, they won't need a scripted step-by-step guide, nor will they be daunted when a component of the plan is curtailed. In the case of the response to the bombings, we had spent much time establishing a process and protocol for designating which hospital each patient would go to; it would be done by a loading officer, who would be able to assign patients across the hospitals allowing for even distribution. With the two blast sites, the rapid load and go of patients and more than one transport location, the mechanism by which patients were assigned hospitals immediately changed to a role managed by CMED at the dispatch center, where additional personnel could support hospital assignments and even distribution across the facilities. This was not a senior command-level decision, this was everyone understanding the essential nature of successful patient distribution and taking necessary action. We have since revised our plans for complex incidents to this format.

Intelligence and Information Sharing

Much has been documented and discussed about the importance of strengthening intelligence and information sharing across Federal, State, and local partners, as a consequence of the bombings. In focusing on this priority, it is important to take a broader look at what constitutes the local-level intelligence community. Since 2007, Boston EMS has assigned a seasoned paramedic to the Boston Regional Intelligence Center (BRIC), the city's fusion center. He has benefited from analyst training, offered through Homeland Security investments, although the position itself has always been paid for by Boston EMS. Having a paramedic assigned to the BRIC helps foster routine information sharing, on matters such as narcotic and violence-related incidents, and establishes a trusted partnership for sharing threat intelligence (as permitted). In addition to better connecting our two departments, our paramedic is able to serve as a broader health and medical subject matter expert, allowing for a unique perspective and contribution. There are public health emergencies that police benefit being informed of, public safety matters that may have health and medical consequences, and, given the broad scope of patients seen by medical providers, there is the potential for EMTs, paramedics, doctors, or nurses to identify a potential criminal threat (either within the home of a patient or in their symptoms). Having an established avenue by which information can be shared across the law enforcement and health care community has been proven to have extensive benefit. EMS is uniquely qualified to serve as a bridge between the public safety and health care communities, as it encompasses both.

Looking more specifically within the health care community, we recognized the need for modeling some of the strengths and benefits of an EOC, but with a health and medical focus, allowing the 60-plus health and medical departments in Boston, including hospitals, health centers, EMS' and public health to better coordinate with each other and share information during emergencies. This idea came to fruition when we secured Federal grant funding in 2008 to convert a conference room into a regional Medical Intelligence Center (MIC). Named after a former Boston EMS deputy superintendent, Stephen M. Lawlor, who promoted interagency collaboration, the MIC has shown much value over the years. During the marathon and the week that followed the bombings, health and medical information sharing was supported by public health, hospital, and EMS personnel assigned to the MIC.

Responding to an Unsecure Scene

Every day, EMTs and paramedics risk their lives to save the lives of others, whether it is stepping onto an unprotected ledge, being hit, bit, spit on, or even shot at. We do what we can to protect our personnel, they are trained in self-defense, they are assigned personal protective equipment, including ballistic vests, but ultimately, when they sign up for the job they understand there is a certain amount of risk. When a representative from Israel, who came to speak at a conference we hosted, was asked how they sent their personnel into unsecure scenes, knowing the risk of secondary devices, he explained that "you do everything you can to prepare them, you try to get them in and out as quickly as possible, but ultimately, this is the job they signed up for." The safety of our personnel will always be paramount, but when everything they are taught focuses on caring for the injured, we can expect that they will respond. This is what happened on April 15, everyone knew the risk and they responded. Ensuring EMS personnel across the country receive necessary training and personal protective equipment is now being recognized more broadly as a priority.

Planning for Others to Respond

Just as we can expect first responders to enter unsecure scenes when there are people in need of medical care and transport, we should also plan for members of the public to respond, as we saw on April 15. The skills of those who assisted varied, although not having a public safety or medical background was not necessarily a limitation, many asked what they could do; some were instructed on the application of tourniquets and others served vital roles in supporting patient movement. During an incident as we experienced in Boston, the initial priorities were quite simple: (1) Immediate trauma care, such as the application of a tourniquet, if necessary, (2) extraction to a point where they can be loaded into an ambulance, and (3) transport to a hospital. While assistance can be helpful in the first two steps, it is important to ensure others understand that if their presence hinders any of these elements, it is best if they stay back. Congestion, particularly if it inhibits ingress or egress of ambulances, can have a negative consequence for patient survival. Ultimately, the onus is on us, members of public safety and homeland security, to ensure it is broadly understood that a disaster is defined by the impact to human life and that for those suffering traumatic injuries, rapid ambulance transport is essential. Plans, trainings, protocols, and guidance should focus on supporting these priorities, within the first response and emergency management community, as well as with the public at large.

The Role of EMS Extends Beyond the Immediate Response to Injuries

Boston EMS has been asked to speak of the immediate triage, transport, and distribution of patients in the aftermath of the bombs, but what is less recognized is the role our personnel played in the events that continued throughout the week. Department personnel were assigned to the blast site for the duration of the road closure and every public event that occurred to honor those who were injured; we worked in partnership with the Boston Police Department, were on scene during each of the captures, and transported both suspects.

The Value of Experienced Personnel

At Boston EMS, our EMTs have an average of 10 years of experience on the job and our paramedics have 25 years. When we invest in training, equipment, and exercises, the experience is applied to an individual member of the department. Over time, this investment, coupled with the skills they garner from years on the job, becomes a tremendous asset to the department and the city they serve. By focusing on EMS as a career, by fully recognizing EMTs and paramedics as public safety officers, we make our communities better prepared for potential emergencies of any scale. Boston EMS had over 140 department members provide direct care to those injured by one or both of the blasts, either directly on scene or while in transport. Even more were involved with events that transpired over the following week. Just the one day, April 15, represented more traumatic injuries than people with more than 30 years on the job have ever seen. In the aftermath of the experience, Boston EMS' sick time went down and the injury rate went down, people worked harder and worked through what might otherwise have kept them out, because they knew they were needed. Having dedicated and highly-qualified EMS personnel is something we hope our experience will lend broader recognition and appreciation for Nationally. Just as we need career police officers and fire fighters, we need career emergency medical technicians and paramedics.

CAPTURING LESSONS LEARNED

Boston EMS hosted two compensated internal 4-hour after-action meetings open to all personnel on May 2, 2013, during the day and evening shift. A paramedic was assigned to perform more in-depth one-on-one interviews to capture additional feedback. Personnel were asked to submit any additional comments verbally or in writing, if desired. An interagency meeting with our private EMS partners, as well as attending hospital after-actions, helped us draw from and better understand their experiences. A number of other after-action meetings took place within the city and State.

INCORPORATING LESSONS LEARNED TO IMPROVE PREPARATION AND RESPONSE TO FUTURE (OR POTENTIAL FUTURE) EVENTS

When we read about and spoke to the first responders from other communities who had just experienced a natural disaster or terrorist attack, we thought through what we would have done in a similar situation, but also understood that we should add any new best practices to our overall all-hazards approach. There were no planes that attacked us, no floods, no chemical agents or structural collapse, but there were many lessons learned we applied from 9/11, Hurricane Katrina and Sandy, the Tokyo Sarin attacks, earthquakes, and tornadoes. It is our hope that others hearing about our story, look beyond the possibility of a bombing and draw from the many other practices that will save lives regardless the nature of the disaster.

More than anything, the experience validated much of what we were already doing. Certain measures wound up working well in response to the bombs; if they were not already built into plans, they now are. In talking to others, we also learned how their plans were influenced by expectations we had established. For example, we spent many years coordinating and exercising with hospital partners; this experience reinforced the fact that during mass casualty incidents, EMS would use triage tags. They grew to expect this and made the determination that triage classifications assigned by EMS would be an initial guide for prioritizing patients upon receipt. When the first patients did not have triage tags, this had a direct impact on the hospitals that we had never expected. While the most critical patients were transported first, this was an important lesson learned, reinforcing the fact that we are integrally connected in the continuum of patient care. Steps have now been taken to forward-deploy triage tags during special events, to increase the likelihood that tags will be applied to patients from the onset, should it become necessary.

SHARING LESSONS LEARNED

To date, presentations and speaking panels have been the principal means for communicating our experience, although we hope to complete an official after-action report. Homeland Security funding was utilized to fund a Massachusetts After-Action and Improvement Plan.

THE ROLE OF THE FEDERAL GOVERNMENT

Boston EMS has long benefited from Department of Homeland Security funding, particularly Urban Areas Security Initiative grants, which have paid for training, exercises, and equipment. As a regional grant, it has helped foster regional and interdisciplinary coordination and standardization. That said, there is currently no requirement to use any homeland security grant funding to support EMS. While we have been fortunate to have a supportive emergency management office that includes EMS, we have not seen that to be consistent when we speak to our partners in other parts of the country. We commend FEMA for making emergency victim care a priority, but ultimately, without directly tying priorities to funding and required outcomes, it is at the discretion of the local and State recipients whether or not sufficient investment is made to strengthen such capabilities. The funding has been invaluable, but the more it can focus on promoting inter-disciplinary and inter-jurisdictional coordination, the better a community will be prepared to handle disasters of all scale and scope.

RECOMMENDATIONS TO CONGRESS

I would also ask Congress to continue support to the UASI program as it has proven value. Recognizing that disasters do happen, as much as we try to protect against them, it is imperative that homeland security be inclusive of EMS and the broader health care community. EMS as a discipline and as a critical function needs to be viewed within the lens of public safety for the purpose of homeland security. In doing so, there will be life-saving benefits on a daily basis, as well as during disasters. The fact that emergency medical services may be different in each city or town, should not diminish the importance of the function and discipline; emergency victim care is vital in any disaster; EMTs and paramedics who operate ambulances are the first responders.

I wish to thank Chairman Michael T. McCaul, Ranking Member Bennie G. Thompson, the Members of the committee, Boston Mayor Martin J. Walsh, and the executive director of the Boston Public Health Commission, Dr. Barbara Ferrer for allowing me to submit this written testimony.

Chairman MCCAUL. Thank you, Chief Hooley. Let me again commend you for your life-saving, heroic measures that day in Boston.

Chairman now recognizes Dr. Jackson.

STATEMENT OF BRIAN A. JACKSON, DIRECTOR, RAND SAFETY AND JUSTICE PROGRAM, THE RAND CORPORATION

Mr. JACKSON. Thank you.

Chairman McCaul, Ranking Member Thompson, and Members of the committee, thank you for inviting me to testify this morning and to be part of such a distinguished panel.

In my written testimony I address three areas where Congress can play a significant role in maintaining the National preparedness and response system that supports first responders to future incidents, and which lessons from past response operations indicate should still be important priorities: The need for better ways to assess and measure preparedness, continuing to support and improve upon programs that protect emergency responders' health and safety at large-scale incidents, and improving the adaptability and agility of the National response system by more effectively learning lessons from the preparedness exercises that we have heard about held at the local level to tell us about the National response system.

Action in these areas via Congressional support and oversight could contribute to better preparing the country to contain the human and financial costs of future attacks, incidents, and natural disasters. In my oral remarks I will focus on the first two of these.

The men and women of the fire service, law enforcement, emergency medical services, and the wide range of other Government and non-Government organizations that are called on for often large and very complex response operations are absolutely central to the Nation's ability to deal with a future that will always be uncertain and will always hold the risk of terrorist attack, natural disaster, and other damaging incidents.

These organizations play that role while also responding to the much smaller-scale everyday emergencies that affect their jurisdictions and populations, the demands of which already stretch some of these organizations' resources.

To enable responders to do their jobs during large-scale incidents and attacks it is critical that the National Preparedness System, from the Federal to the local level, work together and support them effectively. Concerns regarding the performance of that system led to substantial legislative and executive actions in the wake of both September 11 and the Hurricane Katrina in 2005.

Performance at subsequent response operations has demonstrated that these actions have produced significant improvements in National preparedness, and the contrast between well-executed recent responses like Boston or to Hurricane Sandy and to Hurricane Katrina is striking.

However, trends in both the future risk environment—particularly increasing numbers of large-scale, response-intensive natural disasters—and a challenging fiscal environment, that we have heard about, is putting pressure on response organizations, emphasize the importance of continued focus on the health and functioning of the National response system. Given such challenges, there are areas where Congressional focus would be valuable, and I will discuss two of these that have been the subject of significant RAND research.

First, the issue of improved evaluation and preparedness assessment. To support first responders at large incidents there needs to be a clear picture of the capabilities of the National Preparedness System. Significant strides in preparedness measurement have been made since 2001 by both the Department of Homeland Security and the Department of Health and Human Services, but this is not yet a solved problem, as recent GAO reports have highlighted.

Effective measures are necessary to have confidence that the National Preparedness System will be able to support first responders and also to educate the public about what they should and should not expect when disaster strikes. Measurement becomes even more critical under fiscal austerity, since without good measures it is difficult to have an educated public debate about preparedness and make trade-offs with a clear understanding of the implications of funding allocation choices.

Second, protecting the safety of emergency responders. Responders clearly take risks as the assist others, and the Nation relies on them to do so. Providing both the necessary equipment and safety management structures to minimize risk to them is not just the right thing to do, it is in the Nation's interest as well.

The experience of 9/11 and the extensive health impacts on many responders to those attacks have demonstrated the significant personal, organizational, and financial costs that can result. Since 2001 there has also been major progress on improving safety management for response operations, coming out of focused efforts to learn from those responses and others.

There have been broad efforts involving a wide range of organizations to improve both the doctrine and practice of safety management, including processes for monitoring health and safety of responders before, during, and after deployment at large-scale response operations. However, the experience at the Deepwater Horizon oil spill response and cleanup has shown that challenges remain.

In conclusion, the Nation obviously relies on first responders to act and act effectively when major incidents and terrorist attacks occur while simultaneously responding to all of the emergencies that occur on a daily basis. For the Nation to be prepared for large-scale events, the National Preparedness System needs to effectively support those initially local responders who will always be the first ones on the scene.

Again, Chairman McCaul, Ranking Member Thompson, and Members of the committee, thank you for inviting me to submit testimony on this important issue.

[The prepared statement of Dr. Jackson follows:]

STATEMENT OF BRIAN A. JACKSON [1][2]

JUNE 18, 2014

Chairman McCaul, Ranking Member Thompson, and Members of the committee, thank you for inviting me to testify this morning and to be a part of such a distinguished panel.

Today I am going to talk to you about three areas where Congress has a significant role in maintaining the National preparedness and response system that supports first responders to future incidents—and where lessons from past response operations indicate a continuing need for focused attention:

- Developing better ways to assess and measure preparedness to maintain both responders' and public confidence that the National preparedness system will be there when they need it;
- Improving the adaptability and agility of the National response system by more effectively learning lessons from preparedness exercises;
- Continuing to support and improve upon capabilities and programs that protect emergency responders' health and safety at large-scale incidents and disaster responses.

Action in each of these areas—via Congressional support and oversight—can contribute to both better supporting responders to future incidents and to better pre-

---

[1] The opinions and conclusions expressed in this testimony are the author's alone and should not be interpreted as representing those of RAND or any of the sponsors of its research. This product is part of the RAND Corporation testimony series. RAND testimonies record testimony presented by RAND associates to Federal, State, or local legislative committees; Government-appointed commissions and panels; and private review and oversight bodies. The RAND Corporation is a non-profit research organization providing objective analysis and effective solutions that address the challenges facing the public and private sectors around the world. RAND's publications do not necessarily reflect the opinions of its research clients and sponsors.

[2] This testimony is available for free download at *http://www.rand.org/pubs/testimonies/CT211.html*.

paring the country to reduce the human and financial costs of future attacks, incidents, and natural disasters.

The major incidents the country has faced in recent years—including both terrorist attacks and others—clearly demonstrate the critical role played by first responders in containing such events and addressing their consequences. The men and women of the fire service, law enforcement, emergency medical services, and the wide range of other Government and non-Government organizations that are called on for often large and very complex response operations are absolutely central to the Nation's ability to deal with a future that will always be uncertain and always hold the risk of terrorist attack, natural disaster, and other damaging incidents. And the responder community plays that role while responding on a daily basis to the much smaller scale, every day emergencies that affect their jurisdictions and the populations they protect, the demands of which already stretch some of these organizations' available resources.[3]

To enable responders to do their jobs during future large-scale incidents and attacks, it is critical that the National preparedness system—from the Federal to the local level—work together and support them effectively. Concerns regarding the performance of that system led to substantial legislative and executive actions in the wake of both the September 11, 2001 attacks and Hurricane Katrina in 2005. Performance at subsequent response operations has demonstrated that those actions have produced significant improvements in National preparedness.[4] The contrast between well-executed recent responses like those in Boston or to Hurricane Sandy and the response to Hurricane Katrina is striking.

However, two trends emphasize the importance of continued focus on the health and functioning of the National response system:

- The first is that responders' tasks and missions are not getting any easier over time. Statistics on large-scale natural disasters requiring substantial response efforts show an increasing trend, requiring more extensive—and more expensive—response operations.[5] Concern about terrorist attacks has also remained prominent in the years since 2001, with cases like the attacks in Boston demonstrating the unique response challenges of such incidents. First-responder organizations have also been challenged by other incidents of mass violence, with their own distinct response demands.

- Second, the Nation has also just gone through the most serious financial and economic crisis in recent history. During and after the crisis, fiscal austerity at the State and local level drove reductions in budgets of responder organizations—with predictable effects.[6] In recent years Federal spending in this area has also declined,[7] and there is significant concern about controlling Federal expenditures going forward. Though a robust debate about the right amount to spend on preparedness efforts is worthwhile and appropriate, resource constraints nonetheless do represent a challenge to maintaining and further strengthening National preparedness.

Given such concerns about both the future risk and fiscal environment, there are areas where Congressional focus on the National preparedness system would be valuable. I will highlight three that have been the subject of significant RAND research:

- *Improved evaluation and preparedness assessment.*—To support first responders to major incidents, there needs to be a clear picture of the capabilities of the National preparedness system. Department of Homeland Security (DHS) and

---

[3] For example, Kellerman, A.L., *What Should We Learn from Boston?* CT–395, Santa Monica, CA: RAND Corporation, 2013.

[4] Department of Homeland Security, Office of the Inspector General, "FEMA's Preparedness for the Next Catastrophic Disaster—An Update," OIG–10–123, September 2010; Dodaro, G.L., "Department of Homeland Security: Progress Made and Work Remaining in Implementing Homeland Security Missions 10 Years after 9/11," GAO–11–940T, September 8, 2011.

[5] Smith, A.B. and R.W. Katz, "US billion-dollar weather and climate disasters: data sources, trends, accuracy and biases," *Natural Hazards*, Volume 67, Issue 2, 2013, pp. 387–410; Department of Homeland Security, Office of the Inspector General, "FEMA's Preparedness for the Next Catastrophic Disaster—An Update," OIG–10–123, September 2010; Kostro, S.S., A. Nichols, A. Temoshchuk, "White Paper on U.S. Disaster Preparedness and Resilience: Recommendations for Reform," Washington, DC: CSIS, August 27, 2013.

[6] Department of Justice, Office of Community Oriented Policing Services, "The Impact of the Economic Downturn on American Police Agencies," October 2011; Police Executive Research Forum, "Policing and the Economic Downturn: Striving for Efficiency Is the New Normal," February 2013; Cooper, M., "Struggling Cities Shut Firehouses in Budget Crisis," *New York Times*, August 26, 2010.

[7] Pines, J.M. et al., "Value-Based Models for Sustaining Emergency Preparedness Capacity and Capability in the United States," The Institute of Medicine Forum on Medical and Public Health Preparedness for Catastrophic Events, January 2014.

Department of Health and Human Services (DHHS) have made significant strides in preparedness measurement since 2001, including the development of the *National Preparedness Report and the National Health Security Preparedness Index*.[8] Efforts by nongovernmental organizations and analysts have also contributed.[9] Nonetheless, recent reviews by the Government Accountability Office have identified areas where improvement is needed.[10] That this is not yet a fully-solved problem should not be a surprise, given the complexity of evaluating the ability of diverse sets of response organizations across the country to come together and effectively respond to incidents as varied as floods, active-shooter incidents, and bioterrorist attacks. Work at RAND on these challenges has argued that evaluations must distinguish between response systems' theoretical capacity to respond (based on the resources that have been put in place) and whether they will be able to reliably deliver capabilities in the uncertain post-disaster environment.[11] Though much more difficult to measure, it is the ability to reliably deliver capability that is the true measure of preparedness. The need for measurement is tied to good Government goals, including the effective management of Federal investments in preparedness.[12] But the need for preparedness measurement goes beyond questions of management and accountability. Measures are necessary to have confidence that the National preparedness system will be able to support first responders in the future, and to educate the public about what it should—and should not—reasonably expect when disaster strikes. Measurement becomes even more critical under fiscal austerity, since without good measures it is difficult to have an educated public debate about preparedness and make trade-offs with a clear understanding of the implications of funding allocation choices.

- *Supporting agility and continuous improvement in the preparedness system.*— Maintaining preparedness in the face of evolving risks requires mechanisms for identifying lessons from past response operations and applying them to improve preparedness Nation-wide. However, just relying on what we can learn from actual response operations is not enough to adequately prepare for uncertain future threats.

Exercises and drills—for example, those carried out under the DHS' Homeland Security Exercise and Evaluation Program [13] or DHHS' public health preparedness cooperative agreements [14]—are held as part of individual jurisdictions' pre-

---

[8] Maurer, D.C., "National Preparedness: FEMA Has Made Progress, But Additional Steps Are Needed to Improve Grant Management and Assess Capabilities," GAO–13–637T, June 25, 2013; Department of Homeland Security, "National Preparedness Report," March 30, 2013; Centers for Disease Control and Prevention, "Public Health Preparedness: Mobilizing State by State," February 2008; "National Health Security Preparedness Index," on-line at *http://www.nhspi.org/*

[9] For example, National Association of County and City Health Officials, "Indicators of Progress in Local Public Health Preparedness," May 2008.

[10] Jenkins, Jr., W.O., "Measuring Disaster Preparedness: FEMA Has Made Limited Progress in Assessing National Capabilities," GAO–11–260T, March 17, 2011; Caldwell, S., "Homeland Security: Performance Measures and Comprehensive Funding Data Could Enhance Management of National Capital Region Preparedness Resources," GAO–13–116R, January 25, 2013; Maurer, D.C., "National Preparedness: FEMA Has Made Progress, But Additional Steps Are Needed to Improve Grant Management and Assess Capabilities," GAO–13–637T, June 25, 2013.

[11] Jackson, B.A., *The Problem of Measuring Emergency Preparedness: The Need for Assessing "Response Reliability" as Part of Homeland Security Planning*, OP–234–RC, Santa Monica, CA: RAND Corporation, 2008; Nelson, C. et al., "Conceptualizing and Defining Public Health Emergency Preparedness," *Am J Public Health*, Volume 97 (Suppl 1), 2007, pp. S9–S11; Jackson, B.A., K.S. Faith, H.H. Willis, "Are We Prepared? Using Reliability Analysis to Evaluate Emergency Response Systems," *Journal of Contingencies and Crisis Management*, Volume 19, Issue 3, 2011, pp. 147–157; Jackson, B.A., K.S. Faith, H.H. Willis, *Evaluating the Reliability of Emergency Response Systems for Large-Scale Incident Operations*, MG–994–FEMA, Santa Monica, CA: RAND Corporation, 2010; Jackson, B.A., K.S. Faith, "The Challenge of Measuring Emergency Preparedness: Integrating Component Metrics to Build System-Level Measures for Strategic National Stockpile Operations," *Disaster Medicine and Public Health Preparedness*, Volume 7, Issue 1, 2013, pp. 96–104.

[12] "Are We Prepared? Measuring the Impact of Preparedness Grants Since 9/11," Hearing Before the Senate Committee on Homeland Security and Governmental Affairs, Subcommittee on Emergency Management, Intergovernmental Relations, and the District of Columbia, June 25, 2013, on-line at *http://www.hsgac.senate.gov/subcommittees/emdc/hearings/are-we-prepared-measuring-the-impact-of-preparedness-grants-since-9/11*.

[13] "Homeland Security Exercise and Evaluation Program," *https://www.llis.dhs.gov/hseep*.

[14] "Funding and Guidance for State and Local Public Health Departments," *http://www.cdc.gov/phpr/coopagreement.htm*.

paredness programs.[15] Beyond just contributing to bolstering preparedness where they are held, such exercises can be a source of insight into preparedness more broadly to guide National improvement efforts. In past RAND work examining exercise design, we have developed and recommended approaches to make it possible for exercises to produce more useful information to inform assessment and improvement efforts.[16] Similarly, our research analyzing the after-action reports from both exercises and incident response operations has demonstrated they too can be a source of insights—a source which to date has not been fully utilized—on the health of the National preparedness system.[17] Measuring the effectiveness of efforts to disseminate lessons learned to the many organizations within the National response system (e.g., *DHS's Lessons Learned Information Sharing System*[18]) also merits attention—since lessons not effectively disseminated and applied are not actually lessons learned from a system perspective.

- *Protecting the safety of emergency responders.*—Lessons learned from past response operations have also demonstrated the importance of providing first responders at major incidents the protection they need to fulfill their critical roles. Responders clearly take risks as they assist others, and the Nation relies on them to do so. Providing the necessary equipment and safety management structure to minimize risks to them is not just the right thing to do, it is in the Nation's interest as well. The experience of September 11, 2001 and the extensive health impacts on many responders to those attacks have demonstrated the significant personal, organizational, and financial costs that can result from the risks involved in some response operations.

  Since 2001, there has been significant progress on improving safety management for response operations, coming out of focused effort to learn from past responses. RAND, in collaboration and with the support of the National Institute for Occupational Safety and Health, facilitated a set of research projects to gather responder safety lessons from those and previous response operations.[19] The resulting products have contributed to broader efforts involving many organizations and agencies to significantly improve responder safety management doctrine and practice,[20] including processes for monitoring the health and safety of responders before, during, and after deployment at large-scale response operations.[21] However, the experience at incidents such as the *Deepwater Horizon* oil spill response and clean-up[22] has shown that challenges remain in effectively protecting responders at large-scale incidents.

---

[15] For example, Dausey, D.J., J.W. Buehler, N. Lurie, "Designing and conducting tabletop exercises to assess public health preparedness for manmade and naturally occurring biological threats," *BMC Public Health*, Volume 7, 2007, pp. 92–101; Biddinger, P.D. et al., "Public Health Emergency Preparedness Exercises: Lessons Learned," *Public Health Reports*, Volume 125 (Suppl 5), 2010, pp. 100–106.

[16] Jackson, B.A., and S. McKay, "Preparedness Exercises 2.0: Alternative Approaches to Exercise Design That Could Make Them More Useful for Evaluating—and Strengthening—Preparedness," *Homeland Security Affairs*, Volume VII, 2011; Nelson, C. et al., *New Tools for Assessing State and Local Capabilities for Countermeasure Delivery*, TR–665–DHHS, Santa Monica, CA: RAND Corporation, 2009; Jones, J.R., et al., "Results of Medical Countermeasure Drills Among 72 Cities Readiness Initiative Metropolitan Statistical Areas, 2008–2009," *Disaster Medicine and Public Health Preparedness*, Volume 6, Issue 4, 2012, pp. 357–362; Jackson, B.A., K.S. Faith, "The Challenge of Measuring Emergency Preparedness: Integrating Component Metrics to Build System-Level Measures for Strategic National Stockpile Operations," *Disaster Medicine and Public Health Preparedness*, Volume 7, Issue 1, 2013, pp. 96–104 (and references therein).

[17] Faith, K.S., B.A. Jackson, and H. Willis, "Text Analysis of After Action Reports to Support Improved Emergency Response Planning," *Journal of Homeland Security and Emergency Management*, Volume 8, Issue 1, December 2011 (see also more recent similar work by others in Savoia, E., F. Agboola, P.D. Biddinger, "Use of After Action Reports (AARs) to Promote Organizational and Systems Learning in Emergency Preparedness," *Int. J. Environ. Res. Public Health*, Volume 9, 2012, pp. 2949–2963.)

[18] "Lessons Learned Information Sharing," *https://www.llis.dhs.gov/*.

[19] Jackson, B.A., et al., *Protecting Emergency Responders: Lessons Learned from Terrorist Attacks*, CF–176–OSTP/NIOSH, Santa Monica, CA: RAND Corporation, 2002; Jackson, B.A., et al., *Protecting Emergency Responders, Volume 3: Safety Management in Disaster and Terrorism Response*, MG–170–NIOSH, Santa Monica, CA: RAND Corporation, 2004.

[20] For example, "National Response Framework," *http://www.fema.gov/national-response-framework*; "Emergency Response Resources," *http://www.cdc.gov/niosh/topics/emres/responders.html*; "Emergency Preparedness and Response," *https://www.osha.gov/SLTC/emergencypreparedness/*; National Response Team, "Health and Safety," *http://www.nrt.org/*.

[21] "Emergency Responder Health Monitoring and Surveillance," *http://www.cdc.gov/niosh/topics/erhms/*.

[22] Kitt, M.M. et al., "Protecting Workers in Large-Scale Emergency Responses: NIOSH Experience in the Deepwater Horizon Response," *Journal of Occupational and Environmental Medicine*, Volume 53, Number 7, July 2011, pp. 711–715; Michaels, D. and J. Howard, "Review of

The Nation relies on first responders to act, and act effectively, when major incidents and terrorist attacks occur—and to do so while simultaneously responding to the much smaller-scale emergencies and crises that occur on a daily basis. For the Nation to be prepared for large-scale events, the National preparedness system—made up of agencies and individuals from the Federal to the local level, inside and outside Government—needs to effectively support the initially local responders who will always be the first on the scene.

Congress, through its oversight role, can contribute to strengthening both the efficiency and effectiveness of the National preparedness system by continuing to support and to encourage agency programs focused on improved preparedness measurement and evaluation, increasing focus on improving the value and effectiveness of preparedness exercises, and supporting on-going efforts to improve protection of responders at large-scale response operations.

Again, Chairman McCaul, Ranking Member Thompson, and Members of the committee, thank you for inviting me to submit testimony on this very important National issue.

Chairman MCCAUL. Thank you, Dr. Jackson.

Chairman recognizes himself for 5 minutes for questions.

Commissioner Miller, you and I discussed in the back room about the rising threat that we see. It seems like with every briefing I get the threat seems to be getting worse overseas, and I believe that with that, too, comes a greater threat to the homeland.

One only need turn on the television today to realize what we have realized for the past year, and that is there is a growing al-Qaeda presence and training ground in Syria and Iraq that I believe is rivaling if not surpassing what we saw in Pakistan and Afghanistan. ISIS—and it very much concerns me.

We are very privileged to have someone from New York; Arlington, where the Pentagon was struck; and of course, Boston—the three biggest targets that we have seen on 9/11 and since then. So we have your expertise, I think, to draw on.

The biggest complaint after 9/11 was we were not connecting the dots, we were not sharing information. Then a decade later we had Boston, and I was disappointed to see that we are still not getting it right.

I had Ed, Ed Davis, the police commissioner, testify that even though he had four members of his police department on the JTTF, that they knew nothing about the Russian warning; they knew nothing about the FBI opening an investigation into Tamerlan; they knew nothing about his travel—foreign travel overseas even though he was on four watch lists. Even though CBP knew about that, we don't know if that was even shared with the entire JTTF or the FBI.

We know in this business we get it right most of the time, but if we don't get it right the consequences can be very, very severe and very damaging, as we saw on 9/11 and in Boston.

So my question to the three of you is: Where are we since 9/11 in terms of this information-sharing process, not only with FBI and DHS but the JTTFs and the fusion centers? Are we where we need to be or can we—do we need to do a better job?

I will start with you, Commissioner.

Commissioner MILLER. Thank you, Mr. Chairman. I would say from New York City's perspective we are in as good a shape as we could be.

the OSHA–NIOSH Response to the Deepwater Horizon Oil Spill: Protecting the Health and Safety of Clean-up Workers," *PLoS Currents*, July 18, 2012.

To take your question in the arc it was delivered, we have a high degree of concern in that there are more foreign fighters in Syria right now in a 3-year war than during the entire pendency of the war with the Russians in Afghanistan the last time, and that is largely owed to the marketing piece of social media that sends out a global message that will bring them there. Twelve thousand of them are—12,000 to 15,000 are estimated to be Westerners from United States, Canada, Europe—visa-waiver countries where they are a plane ticket away from the United States, and that is of great concern.

So within the framing of your question, in that kind of threat environment, when you have to ask yourself, "Will they be hardened, radicalized, trained in weapons and explosives, and who and where will they be when they come back?" Within the structure of the New York City Counterterrorism Program we have the Intelligence Bureau, we have the Counterterrorism Bureau. We have over 100 detectives assigned to the JTTF.

Addressing the issues of my good, close, personal friend, Commissioner—former Commissioner Ed Davis, from Boston, part of the difficulty they had to deal with was that they only had four detectives on the JTTF and that they lived within the threat squad that ran leads. Our investigators are spread out across every single squad in the Joint Terrorism Task Force, so that delivers us a 360-degree view of the activities of that task force across all programs.

Behind that we have a briefer that comes up from the National Counterterrorism Center every week and, within our secured compartment and information facility, conducts Classified briefings for the command staff of intelligence and counterterrorism on the current threat pictures as it is amalgamated in NCTC from overseas, as well as regular briefings that we have between our analysts and the analysts at the FBI.

If anything, Mr. Chairman, the challenge we face is drowning in intelligence, information, and leads in the busy threat stream across a number of platforms. But a lack of connectivity or information sharing is not a New York City problem.

Chairman MCCAUL. That is very encouraging. I do think—I have always said—that the local police and first responders know the streets better than anybody. They are the eyes and ears. I think the FBI can leverage that to their benefit if the information is properly shared.

I do think New York has stood up, and I commend you for your efforts.

Chief Schwartz and Chief Hooley, you are in a little different position. It is more fire fighting, EMS, but I do think there is a benefit to the sharing of information in terms of being prepared.

Like, sir, in Boston I think there was a threat prior to that, not related to Tamerlan, so the—Boston did stand up its EMS operation. I think in Arlington, being so close to the Nation's capital, it would be of benefit, I think for the two of you, can you sort of—can you tell us where you are with information sharing?

Chief HOOLEY. Yes, sir. I definitely think that we are in a better place than we were right after 2001.

You know, Boston started its local regional intelligence center—its fusion center several years ago. In 2007 we did place a full-time paramedic—a veteran person from our department—over there, and that is his primary assignment.

Over the years he has been offered a lot of training that came through DHS for analysis training, has access to the GIS and to other analysts that are in there, is able to sit in on daily briefings, has received a lot of training about, you know, how to handle material and how to pass it on.

Now how—what can be passed on? What comes through is another thing and I can't always speak to that.

But having somebody in there as a trusted partner is a good first step, because sometimes you only need a little bit of lead time to start to put yourself in a position to prepare for something. There was an incident several years ago where I mentioned to one of the staff—you know, I don't think it was anything sensitive; I think it was Law Enforcement-Sensitive—about a truck that was missing, stolen, whatever, up in eastern Canada somewhere that had a large amount of cyanide with it. Again, no threat with it or anything, but just that little bit of information that did come down to us, you know, reviewed our treatment, signs, and symptomology for that, our stores of the antidote that we had, what P.V. do we need to effectively care for people. So it gave us the ability quietly, behind the scene, for the managers and the medical directors to be ready for that.

So again, nothing happened. It didn't evolve. But having that—having people in places like that does give us that early head start.

Chairman MCCAUL. Chief Schwartz, my time is expiring, but if I could touch on interoperability, you mentioned that in your opening statement, that 9/11 Commission recommended greater interoperability. We are still not there. Congress has acted, as well, and there is a $7 billion initiative called FirstNet to develop that interoperability.

Do you feel that the first responders have been adequately consulted with regarding the development of FirstNet?

Chief SCHWARTZ. Congressman, I would say that, you know, so far the efforts at FirstNet are still maturing. We are not too far down the road yet, you know, in terms of results.

But I think that we are confident, you know, to date that we are being consulted. Chief Jeff Johnson, former president of the International Association of Fire Chiefs, is on the board. He is doing a great job, along with some of his colleagues, to do a lot of outreach and inform local communities, local leaders about what this is going to mean.

So I don't think we are too far along yet, but I think we are pleased with where we are to date. We are watching it very closely.

Chairman MCCAUL. That is certainly good to hear.

Chairman now recognizes the Ranking Member, Mr. Thompson.

Mr. THOMPSON. Thank you very much, Mr. Chairman.

I really appreciate the expertise that our witnesses bring to this hearing.

Chief Schwartz and Chief Hooley, the Metropolitan Medical Response System has been credited with building local and regional capabilities to respond to terrorist attacks involving hazardous material and other mass casualty events. However, we have not provided funds for that program since 2011.

Has the lack of this funding, in your professional opinion, affected capabilities for your departments to respond to mass casualty events, and how has your region maintained that capability with the lack of these funds?

Chief SCHWARTZ. Congressman, we have been very fortunate in both Arlington and the NCR to be in an area that receives UASI funding, so it is hard for me to tell you that the amount of money that we were getting with MMRS has been a tremendous loss because we still have other funds coming through the UASI program that enables us to do, you know, some of the same things that we were doing through MMRS.

What I would say is that MMRS, in my estimation, was less about the amount of money that we received; it was more about how it sort-of catalyzed a systems approach to preparedness. It got the right stakeholders to the table to interact around the various threats that a particular community might face and caused them to do planning and the development of capabilities in a way that recognized that everybody has to work together, that there isn't any one profession—or in the case of regional applications, any one jurisdiction—that has, you know, the full solution or a full set of capabilities.

So I would say that in those jurisdictions that, you know, are not the beneficiaries of UASI money, MMRS played a far greater role in getting people to the table even though it didn't provide a lot of money. If I am not mistaken, I think the entire program never exceeded $70 million.

On a local level we were receiving little more than, you know, $150,000 or $200,000 a year. That wasn't buying an awful lot, but it did certainly facilitate getting stakeholders to the table to figure out how to do things together, and that resulted in better performance in the operating environment, in my view.

Mr. THOMPSON. Chief Hooley.

Chief HOOLEY. Congressman Thompson, yes, I really have to echo what I just heard from my new friend here from Arlington. The MMRS program in a lot of ways was the little engine that could.

I think the largest amount of funding we maybe saw in 1 year for that might have been around $300,000. But it did pull together a lot of stakeholders because it was specific to hospitals and to prehospital.

Just to give you a couple of examples from when we did a lot of work with that group to build our staff-sharing agreements between hospitals. We built a lot of our capability to respond to a nerve agent, a chemical attack, and to buy antidote, stockpile that, do the training for that.

We were able to keep that in place, but sustaining that now does mean that we have to draw our other dollars. You either take it from operational money, you take it from UASI, or you don't do it. So that is one of the—our legacies from that.

The other one was we were able to build up a pretty good capability around the medical management of patients if there was a dirty bomb by involving the radiation safety offices from all the hospitals in Boston, who just—the hospitals donate their time to us so we could work on building portals, building other things. They maintain—they keep them available for us to use if there is a mass care event.

So with a small—relatively small investment from MMRS we were able to build some pretty good systems that we are still benefitting from today.

Mr. THOMPSON. My point is sometimes we can provide the seed monies to get people to the table to do something big, and that was kind-of the reason we kind-of pushed those funds.

Dr. Jackson, do you think the Federal Government is doing everything it can to ensure first responders have equipment and technology they need to protect themselves during disaster responses, based on your research?

Mr. JACKSON. Setting the bar at "everything that can be done" is a very high one. I mean, certainly the investments that have been made in the grant programs have built capability over time, sort-of as I cited in my testimony, the change that we have seen since 9/11 and since Katrina really is impressive.

One of the challenges that has come up in our research sort-of trying to understand this from an outside really is the problem of measurement. I mean, some of the things that we have heard about here are the relationships, you know, building the relationship between agencies so they can work together effectively. Figuring out how to measure that to determine, you know, whether the capability that was built between agencies, you know, 5 years ago before staffs change will still be available 5 years from now, you know, when people have retired, when people have been promoted gets to the question about, you know, sort-of how do we ensure that we maintain the preparedness that we have built over time?

So the—sort-of continuing those investments, but also continuing the investments in understanding how to measure it so we know how much confidence we should have in this system is still something that I—that there is a need to focus on at the Federal level.

Mr. THOMPSON. I yield back.

Chairman MCCAUL. Chairman now recognizes the gentleman from New York, Mr. King.

Mr. KING. Thank you, Mr. Chairman.

Let me thank all the witnesses, and especially thank Chief Schwartz for what your department did at the Pentagon attacks of 9/11, Chief Hooley for the outstanding work that the EMS did after the marathon bombings last year. As the Chairman said, it is really amazing that 263 people had severe injuries and no one died. It is really a testament to the outstanding job that you did.

Commissioner Miller, it is good to see you here today. You have a long record in law enforcement—NYPD, FBI, director of National Intelligence Office, and now back with the NYPD.

You know, there is a lot of talk about—excuse me—Federal funding that goes to different police departments around the country, including the NYPD. There are also a lot of unreimbursable expenditures. Can you just give some example—for instance, how many NYPD police officers and civilians are focused on counterterrorism and intelligence?

Commissioner MILLER. As you know, Congressman, one of the things that those funds rarely if ever apply to is personnel costs.

The NYPD's commitment to the counterterrorism mission is second to none in that between those two bureaus we have devoted over 1,000 people to this on a full-time basis, and then pull in additional officers from around the city on ad hoc missions to support the counterterrorism effort every day.

Mr. KING. As you said, that is largely unreimbursable as far as the personnel cost attached to that.

Commissioner MILLER. Yes.

Mr. KING. Right. There are also many threats that are not reported where you have to send detectives out there or officers out there to monitor a situation, which goes unreported but does obviously run up the expenses.

Commissioner MILLER. Yes. That is correct.

Mr. KING. Also, you mentioned about New York being a target. Could you give some examples—for instance, from *Inspire* magazine; rather than just a generic attack on New York, they actually give specific examples?

Commissioner MILLER. New York as a primary target for terrorism is based first on empirical data. When you tick through the 16 plots targeting New York City before and after 9/11, starting with the bombing of the World Trade Center in 1993 and moving forward, but I think when you look at some of the more recent plots, whether it was Najibullah Zazi's plot to put 16 backpacks on the New York City subway system to cause mass casualties or the plot that followed that involving Faisal Shahzad's delivery of a truck bomb to Times Square, both of them would say that they were inspired in large part by the videos and messages of Anwar al-Awlaki.

As you know from your briefings on this committee, Anwar al-Awlaki then aligned himself with a young American from North Carolina via Queens named Samir Khan, who started *Inspire* magazine. From its first issue, *Inspire* magazine has always focused on driving forward—this is an on-line publication of al-Qaeda in the Arabian Peninsula, carrying al-Qaeda's narrative—driving forward the idea of the homegrown terrorist acting out within the capacity of what they could do without the actual support of the headquarters component of al-Qaeda.

We have seen that in a number cases, including Mohammad Quazi Nafis, who drove what he believed to be, as part of an FBI undercover sting operation in concert with the NYPD, a 1,000-pound truck bomb to the front of the Federal Reserve in the middle of a crowded Wall Street lunch hour, and dialed the phone to set that bomb off while watching from a hotel window above six times. When we looked at that device you saw the detonator hooked up to the cell phone with the six missed calls.

In addition, the most recent issue of *Inspire* magazine takes the mistakes that they claim caused Faisal Shahzad's Times Square truck bomb not to function and says that they have remedied those technical errors with a new recipe and instruction manual for a car bomb. The magazine is quite clear in its copy to say that the purpose of this bomb is not to blow up the Federal building, or recreate Oklahoma City, or destroy structures; its specific purpose and design is to kill people in crowded areas. The picture that comes with that accompanying article shows a Ford van coming down

Broadway in Times Square with a red circle on it at the corner of 47th Street and Broadway, which was the same place Faisal Shahzad planted his device.

They suggest actual attacks against New York City right down to citing specific events and crowd conditions that would be optimal. So this is a theme and drum beat that we continue to see.

The Pakistani Taliban has now launched its own magazine called *Azan,* along the *Inspire* model, and it also focuses on attacking within the United States, attacking large cities, specific references to New York City, and urges its readers not to reinvent the wheel. If you can't get a gun, get some other kind of weapon and do what you can.

Mr. KING. Thank you, Commissioner.

Mr. Chairman, if we have a second round I would like to discuss Secure the Cities with Commissioner Miller.

Chairman MCCAUL. Chairman now recognizes in the order of appearance, Mr. Keating, from Boston.

Mr. KEATING. Thank you, Mr. Chairman.

It is great to see you here, Chief Hooley, in particular.

I have a couple questions. One is, quickly, I think one of the most important parts of training is to develop the chain of command so that is there. Could you comment on that? Because in my own experience, when there are emergencies of lesser scale, and you had fire personnel, emergency personnel, police personnel even within the same areas of government, that was a problem.

But how important is that, so that that is established ahead of time?

Chief HOOLEY. Having a chain of command established and having people routinely employ ICS or NIMS is of great importance. When events happen, such as we experienced that day in Boston, people knew—the people I know in my department, and suspect also in police and fire, everyone knew what their positions, duties, and zones of responsibility were that day. They knew who the supervisors were above them.

But they also—the supervisors above them, more importantly, knew how much that they could delegate and let people improvise on the plan to accomplish the mission.

Mr. KEATING. Great. You just segued to one of my other questions from the EMS side.

In the Boston Marathon bombing there was so much that was accomplished through just the good common-sense people exercised. They put people in—not in medical vehicles, many times, but just in cars that weren't equipped, just to get them to the hospital in time.

What lessons were learned from doing that? What resources are necessary in the future? One of the things—things like QuikClot and other things that are there, more accessible to first responders that are important?

Could you comment on what you learned through some of the improvising that occurred and what you saw in terms of the need for additional resources?

Chief HOOLEY. One of the biggest things we saw was, you know, the willingness of the public to step up and become first responders, as well. You know, in a city like Boston, and I am sure in New

York and the Capital Region here, there are a lot of folks who either have medical training, or they have worked in medical settings, they have prior military experience, and they are all willing to step up when they see, you know, fellow citizens injured.

Being able to supply them with quick material—for example, when you mentioned tourniquets, well we have always carried them, we have always deployed them going back many years. You know, now we have since more than doubled that.

All the first responders in Boston now have been equipped with that because we saw just how quick, simple, mechanical tool it is. You know, it requires a minimal amount of training.

Mr. KEATING. So, if I—just jump, because my time is limited, to the panelists as a whole: 9/11 identified one of the most serious needs to be increased communication. In 2012 we have appropriated $13 billion to help that. We have the FirstNet going on; we have—which would be years away.

Where are we now, from your perspective, in terms of increased communication? Because that will save lives. It was identified in the 9/11 Commission report as something that if it had been at a better level would have saved lives.

Where are we now with that communication on the ground?

Chief HOOLEY. Well, for the base interoperability—and I will go real quick—we have made a lot of advances, really thanks to the Federal Government. Our EMTs and paramedics on—just on the radios they carry have hundreds of channels where they can immediately talk to other agencies if they need to, and even the surrounding cities and towns around Boston, all by agreement. There have been a lot of advances there.

The Federal Government also sponsored us being able to build a Boston Area mutual aid network, where we are able to put consoles in the private ambulance companies, because we really depend on the privates to help in a mass care event. If this had been 5 years prior, we would have been forced to go through our rolodex of phone numbers and call companies individually. This way, we hit a button, like on this, we are able to talk to them all.

Mr. KEATING. Great.

Chief Schwartz.

Chief SCHWARTZ. Congressman, I was just going to say, using Virginia as an example, one of the things that we have done is divided—or using the regions that were already established in the Commonwealth of Virginia, and within each of those regions, developed regional interoperability committees that join together both jurisdictions and professions—the different disciplines—to work on the problems, you know, regionally of interoperability. Then the State-wide interoperability coordinator has the role of sort of knitting together what each of those regions is doing.

I think we have made vast improvements in the last almost 13 years now, but, as you say, there is—you know, there is still some work to do. You know, one of the things that I think we need to focus on is that there are an awful lot of jurisdictions out there that simply do not have the resources of a New York of the National Capital Region, and that is where I think we can take greater advantage of sharing infrastructure, you know, that each jurisdiction doesn't necessarily need to build its own capability; it can share infrastructure with other jurisdictions, thereby reducing cost and facilitating interoperability.

Mr. KEATING. Thank you.

My time is up. I yield back.

Chairman MCCAUL. Chairman now recognizes the chair of the Emergency Response and Preparedness Subcommittee, Mrs. Brooks.

Mrs. BROOKS. Thank you, Mr. Chairman, and thank you for hosting this hearing.

Thank you all so very much for what you do.

Good to see you again, Chief Schwartz. You have appeared before our subcommittee and really appreciate you returning.

You have listed, actually, a number of things that you brought up, as well, before the subcommittee. I am curious from your colleagues that are here with you today what are the top priorities that you would like to see fixed. Because you listed a number of things, which I think are very important—security clearances for, whether it is EMS or fire, to sit on JTTFs; over-Classification of Classified information, possibly that issue of over-Classifying information which first responders might very much need to have.

Chief Hooley, you mentioned that you need that information so you can be prepared with respect to antidotes and how to take care of patients, and so forth.

So I am very curious from each of you, what is it that you need? We certainly know that the funding is critically important, but what are the top concerns that you actually have for first responders, particularly with respect to terrorism, which—and as we have heard from the deputy commissioner, with the thousands of people that we are concerned might be returning—thousands of Westerners returning to this country, what are your top priorities?

Deputy Commissioner, just out of curiosity?

Commissioner MILLER. I think you have actually framed it very well. From the New York City standpoint, with the bandwidth we have, though, as has been a bit of a theme behind the questioning here and our testimony submitted for the record, funding is still the top priority in that the counterterrorism overlay, the training that comes with it, the equipment that comes with it, even, as Congressman King pointed out, while we absorb a lot of that cost in the personnel area, the idea of networking the region together, having a common operational picture, getting common operational equipment so we are operating on a common standard—all of this is dependent on the support of the DHS funding, the UASI program, and so on.

The FirstNet issue is critical in that that real estate in the communications world needs to be mapped out, needs to be well-thought-out. Of course, the training, which relates back to the funding.

Mrs. BROOKS. Thank you.

Chief Schwartz, of all the things that you listed, what would be your top priority?

Chief SCHWARTZ. So I am not going to repeat the—you know, what we have all talked about in terms of the funding, but I think, you know beyond the funding there is, you know, dare I call it a behavioral aspect to some of this, you know, what people in positions of leadership are held accountable for.

So as an example, we have talked a little bit about information sharing and, you know, how we at the local level get our information. One of the things that we have discovered is that the people who are amassing that information—the analysts—don't often understand what we do or why we need that information or why it needs to be characterized in a way that would lead us to develop capabilities in response to these threats.

That is why I cite, you know, the Joint Counterterrorism Assessment Team at the NCTC. We have undertaken in the National Capital Region an effort to—something we call Take Your Analyst to Work Day. We actually have the analysts from the intelligence community come out and ride fire trucks, ride ambulances, ride in cop cars so they can see our job, how we do it. It actually makes it clear to them why the information that typically and traditionally they are producing for high-level Federal decision-makers has, in some cases, applicability to us.

Mrs. BROOKS. While that is an incredible example of a best practice, you have also mentioned that we as a country aren't doing a very good job sharing the best practices.

Chief SCHWARTZ. Correct. Correct. We are spending a lot of money on some very good things in our jurisdictional or regional areas, but for all of the money that we are spending, we are not leveraging the best practices.

It seems to me that it would be easy enough in the grant programs to look at some of the success and promote those, incentivize those in subsequent years—adapted for local conditions, obviously, or regional conditions, because not everything is a one-to-one fit. But I think there is not enough out there—not enough awareness of what has worked in other areas.

Patient tracking, as an example. We have heard a couple of times about the Boston experience and other experiences.

In the NCR we have created what we believe is a very robust patient tracking system that overcomes the difficulties of, you know, where patients are during a crisis. How do we promote that beyond our own, you know, marketing of that? How do we get FEMA to say, "This is important and we are going to put money into this so that everybody can enjoy the successes that the National Capital Region has"?

Mrs. BROOKS. Mr. Chairman, because I know that Chief Hooley and Boston have been outstanding in looking at best practices, I could just ask Chief Hooley to respond what—how you have studied best practices, if I am not mistaken, from around the country. Can you share a bit with the committee about that?

With that, I will yield back after his answer.

Chief HOOLEY. Thank you.

You know, we take advantage of every event to try to learn from not only formal after-actions reports that come out later, but whenever we have an opportunity, you know we have expended dollars—sometimes operational dollars or even some grant dollars—to bring some of the folks who dealt with the situations on the ground there in to talk with us.

One example, after Katrina we brought up some folks from the local hospitals and EMS, as well as law enforcement and fire down there, to really give us an idea of what would work, what wouldn't work here to test us. We did that with the Gulf Region for some hospital evacuations.

As it relates to terrorism, we brought over folks from Northern Ambulance Service after their attacks on their subways to find out what worked in the mass care setting, what worked as far as setting up either a field hospital versus getting people out of there. We have talked to people from the Israeli Defense Forces about how to deal with secondary devices, suicide bombers, so that we could maximize our effectiveness if—when our day came.

Mrs. BROOKS. Mr. Chairman, there are so many incredible things that these departments are doing, it just seems that with modern-day technology we as a country ought to be able to figure out how to share these incredible best practices, which I don't think we are doing right now as a country.

With that, I yield back.

Chairman MCCAUL. I completely agree with the gentlelady.

Chairman recognizes now the gentlelady from Texas, Ms. Jackson Lee.

Ms. JACKSON LEE. I thank the Chairman and I thank the Ranking Member for this important hearing.

To all of the witnesses, each of you have had first-hand experience or you have had involvement in the research of this very important component to our National security. Every time I address this question in homeland security I like to use the terminology "National security," because each of you are really on the international front lines, only because many of what you have had to encounter has generated from entities beyond these shores. So I thank you very much for your first-hand knowledge and involvement.

Let me mention the obvious that both the Chairman and the Ranking Member have already made mention of. First of all, I believe the Chairman made mention of ISIS, which is now, in essence, having a large part of Iraq under siege, and as we speak, are moving toward any number of cities and confronting the Iraqi National Security Forces, which are finding it very challenging to deal with these both heinous and violent, horrific, and moral-less terrorists. They represent a threat to Iraq, but the represent the existence of entities that are hungry for publicity and the ability to show their prowess.

We just returned from Nigeria less than 24 hours ago, and you may have heard of something called Boko Haram. Today some would say that that is a small entity in an isolated northeast part of Nigeria, but the delegation that went saw them as vile, moral-less thugs and terrorists that are decapitating police officers, and slitting the throats of women, and kidnapping children. They are connected to the terrorists that are in the Sahel and they are worth taking note of.

I say this because it is well that America has first responders and a new view of intelligence sharing that gives us some comfort since 9/11. But it is always important to be vigilant.

So one of the things that we established—two points—and to my Ranking Member, I support wholeheartedly his analysis regarding using something called all-hazards grants as opposed to the grant process that we had before that would allow the various first responders to seek particular resources and they would be focused on National security and homeland security. I hope that we can continue to work with the administration to see that importance.

I want to read a sentence from Deputy Commissioner Miller, from your statement that said, "That is why it takes additional resources, specialized equipment, and more money to police events that used to simply require police personnel for crowd and traffic control." It is a new day, is it not?

Would you speak to the importance of dollars that impact intelligence sharing and interoperability? I say that because none of you are from the fourth-largest city in the Nation, which is Houston, but we also face our challenges and need to have those resources. But would you speak to that, please?

Commissioner MILLER. I would be pleased to, Congressman Jackson Lee.

The counterterrorism overlay that we referred to, if you look at an event like the Boston Marathon and then you have a major public event, whether it is another race or a major parade, deploying the people who are going to be conducting the countersurveillance in the crowd, looking for operators who might be planning something in the crowd, looking for those Tsarnaev brothers; the deploying of not just a bomb detection canine that is going to look at a package and say "does it contain explosive or not" if it is sitting there, but the more highly-trained and more costly vapor-wake dogs that are going to be able to move through a trail and actually pick up the vapor wake, the unseen odor that only one of those dogs can detect of somebody wearing a backpack or carrying a bag that contains a device moving through a crowd.

When you look in the incredibly scalable world of port security and you want to push that threat outward from a city, the idea of having the sophisticated radiation detective——

Ms. JACKSON LEE. Is very important.

Commissioner MILLER [continuing]. Equipment on your aircraft or on your boats to detect that threat before it enters your port, all of this is enormously costly.

Ms. JACKSON LEE. Chief, may I just thank you.

Chief, may I just ask you the question of interoperability and the importance of having grant dollars to improve interoperability—both the chiefs that are there, between your services and other services?

Chief HOOLEY. Well, it is important—it is important, you know, to maintain it, because as we make advances in communication equipment and we keep expanding our abilities to talk to each other we want to be able to stay current with technologies.

Again, the interoperability then extends beyond us and shared by the public safety agencies. You know, we have built up interoperability now with Mass Highway, so we can talk when—you know, they can direct us from their control centers when there is traffic things with Mass Port for incidents over at the airport. The potential to just keep expanding it, you know, now that you have a base and—is very good.

Ms. JACKSON LEE. Thank you very much.

Chief SCHWARTZ. I would just add that, you know, this entire effort in the wake of 9/11, it seems to me, has been to develop really a National capacity to respond to a crisis, whether it be, you know, terrorism or something more naturally occurring. Every after-action report that has been written has pointed to the issue of communications, the lack of interoperability.

You know, I think the grant money as a way to facilitate people coming together and working on what really are not technological problems, you know, but are problems governance, they are problems of, you know, people sitting down and figuring out what it is they need to get out of the situation, I think is certainly assisted by the grant money to facilitate those relationships.

Ms. JACKSON LEE. I thank the Chairman for his extra time.

I thank the witnesses for that special insight on protecting our National security.

I thank you. I yield back.

Chairman MCCAUL. Thank you.

Chairman now recognizes Mr. Barletta.

Mr. BARLETTA. Thank you, Mr. Chairman.

I appreciate the hard work of our witnesses and the men and women that they represent, who are key members of our communities.

We must train for disasters, and I fully support efforts to train our first responders. As a former mayor for 11 years I know how important this is. I have supported firefighters grants, cops grants, regional information-sharing system. So I certainly understand that.

But we must also prevent—work to prevent a terrorist attack. An ounce of prevention is worth a pound of cure, and my good friend, Michael Cutler, who was an ICE agent, would tell me, "When it comes to terrorism, an ounce of prevention is worth a ton of cure."

Now the best thing that we can do to help our first responders is to prevent a terrorist attack in the first place. Now the 9/11 Commission report was given to Congress to do just that—to make recommendations of what we can do to prevent another attack. It was passed by Congress and signed by the President.

The first paragraph of the preface of the 9/11 Commission staff report on terrorist travel begins with the following paragraph: "It is perhaps obvious to state that terrorists cannot plan and carry out attacks in the United States if they are unable to enter the country. Yet prior to September 11th, while there were efforts to enhance border security, no agency of the United States government thought of border security as a tool in the counterterrorism arsenal. Indeed, even after 19 hijackers demonstrated the relative ease of obtaining a U.S. visa and gaining admission into the United States, border security is still not considered a cornerstone of national security policy."

Now, the 9/11 Commission study on terrorist travel went on to detail numerous examples of instances where terrorists not only made use of visa and immigration fraud to enter the United States, but to also embed themselves in the United States. Page 47 of this report notes, "Once terrorists have entered the United States their next challenge was to find a way to remain here. Their primary method was immigration fraud."

Another paragraph—and this is found on page 98—it said that "terrorists in the 1990s as well as the September 11th hijackers needed to find a way to stay in or embed themselves in the United States if their operational plans were to come to fruition."

Our borders are not secure. We do not have a biometric exit system to identify when someone overstays their visas. We are not enforcing our immigration laws to prevent immigration fraud.

So we have not taken the recommendations of the 9/11 Commission report.

My question is, to each of you: Doesn't this make you nervous?

Commissioner MILLER. From the standpoint of New York City, given all the context we have discussed at this hearing, we go to bed nervous every night, and we wake up nervous every day. It is a state of being in the post-9/11 world.

But to address those concerns, intelligence is, at its simplest, understanding a problem. Good intelligence analysis is understanding it well enough to do something about it. Part of that has to be about being well-placed to collect and analyze——

Mr. BARLETTA. But if I could just—if intelligence tells us that the best way to prevent a terrorist attack is to stop it in the first place, and we know that terrorists use visas as a method of entry into the United States, and we know that they use immigration fraud as a method to embed themselves, wouldn't intelligence then tell us that we should enforce our immigration laws and secure our borders?

Commissioner MILLER. It would be within the Government's capacity to do it. You are asking a local official about a Federal problem, but I think where I was going with that is we have, as well as people in London, Tel Aviv, Oman, Abu Dhabi, Singapore, NYPD people embedded within those services to watch. We also—and I will be meeting with this person after this hearing—have people here at Interpol, but also at Customs and Border Protection.

One of the great relationships we have between the NYPD and the Federal agency, aside from the FBI, is with CBP, in terms of keeping track of who is coming in, making sure that suspects we are investigating aren't getting out, and an alert system that goes both ways on that. I think that between our agencies that works very well.

The larger problem that you frame is beyond the scope of the NYPD to address.

Mr. BARLETTA. Chief Schwartz, does it make you nervous that we are not following this report?

Chief SCHWARTZ. Well, Congressman, I would, you know, echo the commissioner's observations. There is a lot about international travel that, you know, that has me concerned, and that is one element that—you know, the one you are describing is unfortunately one that I have little influence or control over.

As concerning to me is the people, you know, the legitimate people in this country who are, you know, potentially traveling to areas of conflict right now, picking up, you know tactics, techniques, and procedures that they might bring back here and use.

As the commissioner indicates, our ability to get the intelligence on those folks and properly prepare——

Mr. BARLETTA. I understand that. I appreciate that. You know, it is remarkable—the intelligence of what we are able to do, but aren't we missing step No. 1 is to prevent it in the first place? If we can stop an attack from someone even coming here and embedding themselves here, shouldn't that be a priority?

Chief SCHWARTZ. Congressman, I wouldn't argue your point. Absolutely. It is just that from where I sit I have little influence on that.

Mr. BARLETTA. Chief Hooley.

Chief HOOLEY. Well, as you said in the beginning, an ounce of prevention is worth a ton of cure. Can't disagree with that.

I guess, you know, as far as, you know, my influence as a local EMS provider is a little bit—not much when it comes to international travel or those type of matters.

Mr. BARLETTA. But isn't the best thing we could do for the EMS is to not put them in harm's way in the first place?

Chief HOOLEY. Oh, sure. Because our response is based on having to respond to something and consequence management——

Mr. BARLETTA. Thank you.

Dr. Jackson.

Mr. JACKSON. Certainly the challenge here is understanding the right approach to get the most benefit towards this problem. Immigration and border control is one part of that, but as we have heard about, you know, interagency relationships, really this is a systems problem. We have heard discussions about——

Mr. BARLETTA. If you think of enforcing—but again, we are glazing over, because there is a political aspect to this, but there is a National security aspect to this. I get it. I understand the political aspects of it, but I am worried about our National security. We should not be playing politics with the security of the American people.

If we know that terrorists embed themselves in the United States and use immigration fraud as a way to do it, should we be doing that?

Mr. JACKSON. Well, certainly immigration and border protection is one part of this overall system. But there is a resource question here, and it is a question of where in that system an investment in the resources will get the most safety.

Mr. BARLETTA. Isn't the way to get the most safety is to not allow them into the United States in the first place? Seems pretty obvious to——

Mr. JACKSON. In the ideal, depending on what the relative price of getting better there versus getting better——

Mr. BARLETTA. What was the price of 9/11?

Thank you.

Thank you, Mr. Chairman.

Chairman MCCAUL. Time is expired.

The Chairman now recognizes the ever-patient Ms. Clarke, from New York.

Ms. CLARKE. Thank you, Mr. Chairman. It is so good that you should mention that. I just want to put on the record, I got one— you owe me one. Thank you, Mr. Chairman.

To the Ranking Member, as well, thank you.

To our panelists, thank you for sharing your expertise this morning. It has been quite edifying. I think that there are some recurrent themes that, you know, remain a challenge for us.

Let me welcome back the NYPD and welcome back to Capitol Hill Deputy Commissioner John Miller. I wanted to ask—I will start with a question to you, sir—unfortunately, due to the experience of 9/11 and not—and out of the necessity of having thwarted several terrorist attempts since, New York City has developed expertise that serves as a model for counterterrorism planning and programs.

Since you have been in your current position, what counterterrorism programs have you changed, and what programs have you found most effective or ineffective? For example, many Americans in and outside of New York—the New York-New Jersey area—were a bit troubled by a few years back when we learned that NYPD officers were dispatched to New Jersey to conduct surveillance activities at mosques and other social gathering places of Muslim Americans.

In the wake of 9/11 we understand that singling out and targeting individuals based on religion is not the way to go. Violent extremism transcends religion. Can you comment on that?

Then, please share any concerns that your agencies have regarding consolidation of grant programs, maintenance of effort, and its impact on remaining vigilant, stood-up, and forward-leaning in the face of ever-evolving and multi-faceted terrorist threats.

Commissioner MILLER. Let me try and go in order, and if I miss something just bring me back.

As far as concerns about NYPD and the so-called Muslim Surveillance Program, there is nothing called the Muslim Surveillance Program; that is a term kind-of coined by the newspapers so that has become a bit of a bumper sticker. On the other hand, there were concerns about the scope and breadth of NYPD's efforts to gain information at the onset of its intelligence program and its coordination with other jurisdictions.

In the time that I have been back at the NYPD, which is a mere 6 months at this point, what we have done is increase our coordination, I would say in the extreme with the FBI, not just in New York but also in the Newark field division in New Jersey. We have increased an already fairly good coordination with the counterterrorism entity in the attorney general's office in the State of New Jersey.

In terms of the optics issue about, well where were they looking and what were they looking for, part of that is to understand that while jurisdictional borders between law enforcement agencies are critical to be mindful of, both in procedure and in some cases in law, terrorist plotters don't actually honor those borders. The people who built the World Trade Center bomb in 1993 built it in New Jersey. Most of the plot against the Federal Reserve was—the bomb was constructed in Long Island.

So it is incumbent upon the NYPD to have a richer picture in terms of understanding not just New York City but the surrounding areas. Part of the issue there is the community outreach and community relations issues, which is how were those efforts framed? Were the earliest efforts reflective of what we are doing today—and the answer there would be no. I think there was also a bit of a learning curve over those years.

So to get a better understanding and get clearer optics, one of the things that we have done in the past 6 months is to increase our outreach to those communities within the greater metropolitan area. We have had three major meetings with stakeholders in the Muslim community, as well as some of the very groups that are engaged in litigation against us, to bring them to the table, to take their questions, to try and give some answers, to address their concerns.

Today, as we sit here in this room, the New York City Police Department is doing its pre-Ramadan briefing, where they bring in a large number of people from the Muslim community and religious leaders to talk about, before the holiday season, their concerns, from issues as simple as parking during prayer time at mosques to as complex as radicalization—whatever they want to discuss. The police commissioner has met with them personally; I have addressed those concerns, and that is a dialogue we intend to continue.

I just want to close on that issue by saying: Very much in the universe that we lived in in Los Angeles, where we competed with the message of gangs in the streets for the attention of children and teenagers and young people, we are competing with an equally powerful message coming through social media and the publications that go by the narrative of al-Qaeda that is urging young men to travel overseas to fight, to die, to martyr themselves or be maimed or killed, or to come back and bring that narrative back home to the United States.

My message to those stakeholders in the community has been more, "I need a partner here in a counter-narrative to that message that I cannot be the deliverer of the government, the police department, an intelligence entity can't be the one to deliver that message. I need your voices because there is a powerful message coming from the other side and we need to engage in this effort together."

That may mean a little more transparency on my part. I get that, and that is what they are seeking. But I need more help from the community as well.

Ms. CLARKE. I will yield back, Mr. Chairman. Thank you.

Chairman MCCAUL. Thank you. Gentlelady's time has expired.

Chairman recognizes Mr. Payne.

Mr. PAYNE. Thank you, Mr. Chairman, and to the Ranking Member.

To the panel, thank you for your testimony today.

Deputy Commissioner Miller, I know your work with the NYPD. I grew up across the river in Newark, New Jersey, but as a youngster I remember you more on NBC channel four, disseminating information to the community.

Chief Schwartz, I was fortunate enough to have TEEX training in Texas, and they used your experience on 9/11 as the scene, and what you were able to do that day in the circumstances that you found yourself is commendable.

Chief Hooley, to know that you were able to get those people to the hospital within 22 minutes of that function is incredible.

You know, Chief Schwartz, in your testimony, you know that communications problems posed challenges during, you know, the response activities at the Pentagon on 9/11. Can you talk about how States, regions have improved interoperable communication capabilities since 9/11? Can you also talk about the important role of State-wide interoperability coordinators and the regional interoperability working groups?

Chief SCHWARTZ. Thank you, Congressman. I mentioned in a previous question just a little bit about some of the things that we are doing in Virginia with regard to regional groups that are working on the interoperability problem, and that has been facilitated by the State-wide interoperability coordinator, through what, you know, again, as we have talked about in a number of different dimension here, you know, by using some of the grant money as sort-of the hook to get people to the table and get them to cooperate with each other, and it is our hope that, you know, some of the things that we have accomplished there will be continued.

Two other things that we have done in Virginia under the auspices of the interoperability coordinator is to create a linkage between the State's radio system and that of all the local radio systems. The State had a previous architecture that they had invested in, and it was important that, as an example, the State police be able to communicate with local law enforcement, fire, rescue, and so they were able to create a linkage between those two disparate systems.

Then last, and it, you know, it is a relatively, you know, minor issue in the overall scheme of things, but it is not unimportant in the operating environment, and that is the State interoperability coordinator moved everybody towards a common language, which, as you may remember during 9/11, you know, was especially problematic with the use of 10 codes and different terminology that really complicates communication.

So I would just add to this discussion about interoperability that the interoperability can't be seen as, you know, sort-of the Holy Grail. It has to be part of an operating system that includes an effective incident command system, incident management system. In my view, I have seen too many times where interoperability is used as a kind-of a reason not to co-locate and actually make joint decisions.

So I think interoperability needs to be looked at through the lens of operability—you know, the total system of incident management, of which our ability to talk to each other mechanically is but one part.

Mr. PAYNE. Okay. Thank you.

You know, during the discussion, you know, the grants that have been very useful to your different agencies have come up, and, you know, there is a proposal—the NPGP, or the National Preparedness Grant Program—to consolidate UASI and all the grants into one sum of money and have everyone compete. There are many Members in Congress that don't think that is very wise.

I know what UASI has meant to Newark, New Jersey, and to have those dollars all come together and then disseminated to the

State and then, you know, in Newark, cross our fingers and hope that we still continue to get the funding that has been so vital to the success of, you know, our homeland work in Newark that we hope that the State decides, "Well maybe, Newark, you don't need as much." The direct funding to the entities, you know, on the ground is important.

What is your feeling about—of that?

Chief SCHWARTZ. Well, Congressman, we have—you know, both the International Association of Fire Chiefs and and our partner organizations, the professional organizations, I think have been on record. I think this proposal has come forward now three times, and each time we have been of the view that, you know, we don't understand enough about what is trying to be achieved here.

We are concerned about the transparency; we are concerned about—I would say we are concerned about even the competitive nature—the proposal that includes competitiveness, because what we are really trying to do is create a collaborative spirit here, right? How do we build systems in which people can work across the traditional boundaries?

So, you know, I think our position has been not to dismiss it out-of-hand, but not enough information has come forward that gives us the confidence that we can achieve some of the same successes that we have had to date under the proposal that has come forward now a few times.

Mr. PAYNE. Commissioner Miller.

Commissioner MILLER. From the simplest perspective, I have always believed, as the former head of counterterrorism and intelligence for the city of Los Angeles Police Department and now New York City, that the money should go where the threats are and where the targets are. That is a basic principle.

I would also say that one of—reflecting on the chief's comments, one of the great successes of the UASI program in its current form is that it has pushed the money where the threats are, despite the expansion of UASI regions. But it has also at the same time, to Chief Schwartz's point, developed regional partnerships and strategies in how to exploit that money best within the regions where the threats and targets are.

Mr. PAYNE. Thank you.

Mr. Chairman, I will yield back. Thank you.

Chairman MCCAUL. I wasn't planning on opening up to a second round of questions.

Mr. King does have a question, and I would like to recognize him.

Mr. KING. Thank you, Mr. Chairman.

Chairman MCCAUL. Of course, if the other Members would like to, that is fine as well.

Mr. KING. Thank you, Mr. Chairman.

Again, I regret that I had to leave for another meeting, but I just want to follow up on something.

First of all, let me just say, Commissioner Miller, besides being on this committee I am also on the Intelligence Committee. I do get Sensor briefings. When I see the threats and potential threats and possible threats against the city of New York and the outstanding work that you do and the NYPD does, and knowing that people in the community could participate in those threats and how important this is to prevent them and to monitor what is happening, I want to commend the NYPD for respecting Constitutional rights and protecting the safety and liberty of the people of the city of New York.

In that regard, the Secure the Cities program has been funded now for a number of years, and there are questions as to how far into the future that funding should go. I believe it should be extended. I think it is vitally important. But if you could explain the significance of the program and also how that technology is transferable throughout the country?

Commissioner MILLER. The Securing the City program has been vital to the New York City Region, and I say "region" with an underline on the region part. This was a program that started with base funding of $18 million to develop this program where we would have radiation detection across the region. The regional piece is critical because, as the President of the United States said when he was asked an international affairs question recently, he said, "What keeps me up at night is the thought of a nuclear device in New York City. Regional conflicts will come and go."

We have seen that go from $18 million to $16 million to $11.5 million, and then plans to take it down to the $4 million-plus area. Building this out in New York City and then getting the common operational picture through the region, the common operating equipment, the same standards, the same vendors has given us the ability—again, back to the World Trade Center example—you know, they are not going to construct a nuclear device in New York City. It is going to come in through a port; it is going to be built on an off-site—in an area outside New York City, which means that detection equipment radiating out from the urban center that could be a target is critical, and we have built that incrementally over time.

I would like to thank you for your efforts personally for helping us with the Department of Homeland Security and our efforts to maintain that funding as we complete that building process.

To the back end of your question, is how could that help other regions, we were the first to do this regional Securing the Cities thing, with New York City serving as, for lack of a better term, the executive agent and helping the smaller agencies as they radiated out—150 of them within that region. I think what we have learned over time and what we have developed in terms of a program is transferrable.

It is the conversations we have been having with my former colleague in LAPD, Mike Downing, about how to apply those lessons, and form, and format to their efforts, as well as Superintendent Gary McCarthy, in Chicago.

Mr. KING. Thank you, Commissioner.

I yield back, Mr. Chairman. Thank you for the extra time.

Chairman MCCAUL. Thank you.

I want to thank the witnesses.

I would be remiss, Commissioner, if I didn't allow you a few minutes to share with this committee your interview with Osama bin Laden.

Commissioner MILLER. It was something that happened in the last days of May 1998, a few years before September 11, back, I think, before that was within our concept. But I would like to say this: In sum and substance, what Osama bin Laden said to me over the course of an hour sitting face to face in that tent on a mountaintop in Afghanistan was this, that the system is more important than the organization.

When I asked him if he was concerned about being captured or killed by the United States, his answer was, "I am building an organization that is going to outlive me and whoever comes behind me by networking the message and the groups together."

But he also said on May 28, 1998, "I predict a black day for America, after which nothing will be the same, that this war with the United States will be greater than our battle with the Russians, and that you will only come to understand this when you leave our lands dragging your bodies in shameful defeat and the coffins and the boxes."

I think at the time he said those words to me in 1998 it sounded a tad, Mr. Chairman, hyperbolic. Who was this individual who was not the leader of a state nor the general of an army, who had access to funds but not National treasure, to declare war on the United States and to predict that kind of outcome?

I think Chief Schwartz and Chief Hooley and Dr. Jackson would agree that had that interview been done on September 10, 2001 and reviewed later in that week, it would have sent—it would have sounded a lot less hyperbolic.

So from that I take a lesson in context, which is, right now, through the very Classified briefings that you and Congressman King and the other Members of the Homeland Security Committee sit in, we are seeing an unraveling of a security picture that seems very far away in places like Iraq and Libya and Syria, and we are seeing the emergence of a group of new potential Osama bin Ladens who are claiming leadership and ability to extend their reach and power in terms of threat and action.

So I would like to commend my fellow first responders at the table for their continued attention, heroism, and commitment for what they do, because more than a decade after 9/11 the threat stream is not an awful lot brighter and the picture is changing minute-to-minute.

I commend the committee and thank you all, individually and as a group, for the support, perspective, and wisdom you bring to this fight.

Chairman MCCAUL. Well let me just say, sir, thank you for sharing that very powerful story and reminder that the threat is still, unfortunately, very much alive and well.

I see we had one Member show up at the last minute.

Mr. Vela, would you like to be recognized for questions?

Okay.

Did the Ranking Member have any additional questions?

With that, I want to thank the distinguished witnesses for your compelling testimony. It is very helpful to this committee.

Without objection, this committee stands adjourned.

[Whereupon, at 11:57 a.m., the committee was adjourned.]

APPENDIX

QUESTIONS FROM CHAIRMAN MICHAEL T. MCCAUL FOR JOHN MILLER

Question 1a. How can we improve the sharing of information developed in a JTTF to outside organizations, such as State and local law enforcement, and fusion centers?

Answer. This would have to be done very carefully. JTTFs are both collectors and consumers of intelligence, but the primary role of the JTTF is to run investigations. The primary role of fusion centers is not to do investigations (this is always a temptation, because everybody wants to be in the game) but to do analysis and share that. Once a fusion center becomes a detective squad doing investigations, it loses its focus on the analysis role. In the same vein, a JTTF should not become the font of intel to the State and local police units.

Question 1b. Perhaps some sort of integration between JTTFs and fusion centers?

Answer. The best model I have seen is in Los Angeles. The LA Regional Intelligence Center (J–RIC). At the JRIC, they have an "all crimes, all hazards" approach. They deal with crime and CT. This is reinforced by the theory that many terrorist plots had their roots in other crimes. The FBI has embedded the "Threat Squad" there. By doing this, the FBI Threat Squad takes all the incoming threat info and teams up with local officers who run the leads on the ground. This keeps the fusion center in the loop. At the same time FBI analysts are embedded on the Classified side of the fusion center. This way, the JTTF does its job on the main cases. The Threat Squad runs out all the leads keeping the fusion center involved. The fusion center does its job by providing threat info and analysis tailored to the community it serves.

Question 1c. Do you have any other suggestions as to how we can make the best use of the resources in the fusion centers.

Answer. All fusion centers should be "All Threats," meaning they should study, collect, and analyze intel on all crimes.

QUESTIONS FROM CHAIRMAN MICHAEL T. MCCAUL FOR JAMES H. SCHWARTZ

Question 1a. How can we improve the sharing of information developed in a JTTF to outside organizations, such as State and local law enforcement, and fusion centers?

Question 1b. Perhaps some sort of integration between JTTFs and fusion centers?

Question 1c. Do you have any suggestions as to how we can make the best use of the resources in the fusion centers?

Answer. This question concerns the relationship between the JTTFs and fusion centers. As the Nation has invested in the development of fusion centers, it is fair to say that a division of labor or relationship needs to be better defined between the JTTFs and fusion centers. While a few like the Los Angeles JRIC are very good at integrating the fusion center and JTTF missions, my experience is that that is not the case in many fusion centers.

In the National Capital Region (NCR), there are examples of good coordination between the FBI Washington, DC field office and the Northern Virginia Regional Intelligence Center (NVRIC). However, as I testified, there is a long-standing history of the field office working with local fire and EMS departments that could be replicated in all field offices. This relationship was a key component during the response to the 9/11 incident at the Pentagon where critical intelligence was shared in the command post and influenced numerous decisions. Even now, the field office hosts twice-monthly conference calls in which they include the fire chiefs of the NCR to update them on threats and operations. Over the last 13 years every piece of significant information that I have received as a local official, information that caused me to rethink my preparedness efforts, has come from the FBI. Information that which has been provided by the fusion center has in every instance been that already provided by the Bureau or was available in open sources, normally the news media.

It is worth assessing whether the return on investment from fusion centers is worth the cost. More than a decade after their formation across the Nation many fusion centers have shifted the majority of their focus to "all crimes" which may be appropriate given the real but relatively small threat from terrorism when compared to daily crime in many communities. In these centers there is often a close link with the investigation functions separate from the JTTF. Consideration should be given to letting fusion centers focus on local and regional crime, which was the role of criminal intelligence before 9/11, and requiring that when there is a terrorism nexus, the issue be turfed to the JTTF who would then be responsible for coordinating with locals. Additionally the practice of adding fire/EMS representatives to the JTTF as is done in New York and Los Angeles, should become standard practice. Redirecting some of the resources now dedicated to a murky mission in the fusion center to a JTTF would not only facilitate greater information sharing with locals but would also provide the Bureau with an operational perspective many do not currently have.

Question 2a. Many fusion centers have developed Terrorism Liaison Officer (TLO) programs, which are one way "non-traditional partners," including the fire service and EMS, can gain situational awareness on current terrorist tactics, techniques, and practices.

Question 2b. Do your departments have dedicated Terrorism Liaison Officers?

Answer. In general, there are a number of good TLO programs across the Nation. The cities of Phoenix, Arizona and Los Angeles, California probably have the best example of a TLO program.

In NCR, we do not have a TLO program. The Northern Virginia region has placed a fire/EMS representative at the NVRIC and developed a fire chief's intelligence committee that works closely with the fusion center representative. However, fire and EMS participation at the NVRIC is limited to that person. We are not allowed to provide substitutes when the representative takes leave, or add extra staffing (even though the jurisdictions have offered to cover the cost of additional fire and EMS representatives) and there is no executive representation from the fire and EMS community on the NVRIC governing board. This issue can present problems in developing a strong relationship between the fusion center and fire departments that it serves.

Question 2c. Do your local fusion centers provide training to the TLOs on how to properly report suspicious activities that may be observed on call?

Answer. The Arlington County Fire Department developed a suspicious activity reporting (SAR) policy many years ago, and it was adopted by other agencies in the Northern Virginia region. Training has been provided to all personnel in the region. Any suspicious activity is reported to both the Fire/EMS representative at the NVRIC and local law enforcement agencies, which have representatives at the JTTF.

QUESTIONS FROM CHAIRMAN MICHAEL T. MCCAUL FOR JAMES HOOLEY

Question 1a. How can we improve the sharing of information developed in a JTTF to outside organizations, such as State and local law enforcement, and fusion centers?

Perhaps some sort of integration between the JTTFs and fusion centers?

Question 1b. Do you have any other suggestions as to how we can make the best use of the resources in the fusions centers?

Answer. Let me begin by describing the relationship of my department, Boston Emergency Medical Services (Boston EMS), with the local fusion center and the JTTF. Boston EMS is what has been described as a "non-traditional partner" within the Boston Regional Intelligence Center (BRIC), the city's fusion center, located at the Boston Police Department (BPD). Boston EMS has had a paramedic assigned to the BRIC full-time, 5 days a week, since 2007.

Boston EMS is a member of the Massachusetts Anti-Terrorism Advisory Committee, which is co-chaired by the U.S. Attorney for Massachusetts and the SAC of FBI Boston. Although we are not a member of the JTTF, several BPD members from the BRIC, with whom we work with regularly, are assigned to the JTTF. From my perspective, our law enforcement partners at the BRIC are integrated at the JTTF and EMS depends on those officers to represent us at the JTTF, much like other non-traditional partners, such as public health and fire services. I do think that the BRIC representatives to the JTTF would be comfortable sharing information they receive from the JTTF with EMS, as security levels permit. Having said this, I believe the JTTF would be more likely to share information once they determine it necessary. It is my hope that the JTTF's look beyond law enforcement, to understand the threat-intelligence needs of non-traditional partners and how soon they would require this information.

The JTTFs should have regularly scheduled briefings with non-traditional partners. This dialogue would promote better understandings of each other's needs. For example, if a JTTF were to comprehend the capacities, capabilities, or risks to EMS, hospitals, or public health departments, it may influence what information they share and when they choose to do so.

Another suggestion on how to best use resources from fusion centers is to establish practices that streamline the ability to take higher-security classification material and revise it to a level where it can be disseminated to more stakeholders.

As a hypothetical (non-terrorism) example, imagine the FBI or DEA issues a Law Enforcement Sensitive report warning of a serious contamination or additive to illicit drugs being trafficked on the streets. Security requirements would prohibit the representative from sharing this information with non-law enforcement personnel, including EMS field providers, drug outreach workers, hospital emergency department clinicians or poison control center staff. There is a process to review and redact information that would lower it to FOUO, allowing it to be shared at lower levels. Admittedly I am not familiar with the time required for such approval or any remaining limitations on sharing. I would recommend that JTTFs and fusion centers discuss and plan for a process by which information can be shared with necessary public safety, public service, and public health and health care entities, as appropriate, to ensure the right information gets to the right people in sufficient time to meet the desired objective of protecting the public.

Question 2a. Many fusion centers have developed Terrorism Liaison Officer (TLO) programs, which are one-way "non-traditional partners," including the fire service and EMS, can gain situational awareness on current terrorist tactics, techniques, and practices. Do your departments have dedicated Terrorism Liaison Officers?

Question 2b. Do your local fusion centers provide training to the TLOs on how to properly report suspicious activities that may be observed on a call?

Answer. I have read about various Terrorism Liaison Officer programs in other jurisdictions. Boston EMS does not have a dedicated TLO per se, however, our EMS liaison at the BRIC has been offered and received several DHS and other agency-sponsored trainings. This includes but is not limited to analyst trainings, conferences, exercises, training in the proper handling of Classified materials, a security clearance, suspicious activity reporting, and regularly receiving bulletins and briefings that may be of interest to EMS. In his capacity as our representative to the BRIC he will train our personnel in the field on what they should look for and consider reporting. Our EMS representative at the BRIC does not enter SAR data directly into the database. He provides the data to staff at the BRIC who vet the information and decide whether to enter it. The EMS representative will also share information from threat assessments, particularly as they relate to large public gatherings or events, to EMS providers in the Metro Boston Homeland Security Region as well as the hospitals and public health agencies.

Currently, the BRIC is working to develop the TLO concept and bring in more non-traditional partners. I wish to emphasize that although it is important to receive the necessary training and clearances to participate in a fusion center; those are only the first steps. To be truly effective as a member of a fusion center, law enforcement and non-traditional members must be trusted members of the team. They should be present for the daily briefings. They should have access to analysts, GIS specialists, the Sensitive Compartmented Information Facility when needed and other resources at the fusion center, as our EMS representative has. Developing that relationship as a trusted agent in a fusion center will enhance the likelihood that critical information is shared and utilized, not merely collected.

QUESTIONS FROM HONORABLE SUSAN W. BROOKS FOR JAMES HOOLEY

Question 1. In 2012, FEMA reduced the period of performance for grants from 3 years to 2 in an effort to address the amount of funding that had yet to be drawn down by grant recipients. Has the reduction in the period of performance had an impact on your ability to expend the grant funds on projects that truly address your capability gaps?

Answer. The FEMA-reduced period of performance for grants from 3 years to 2 has presented a significant challenge to the Metro Boston Homeland Security Region, negatively impacting the ability to develop and sustain core capabilities. This approach is creating a bias towards buying more assets, rather than implementing the life-cycle planning envisioned by the National Preparedness Goal.

Prudent grant management requires extensive procedures allowing for accountability and compliance as funding is transferred from the Federal level to the State, from the State to the region, and then from the region to a local department or a vendor, in addition to EHP reviews. While each step is in many respects essential, they can create time-consuming delays and chokepoints.

With each investment, extensive effort is placed on determining how best to spend the grant dollars. Regrettably, a 2-year grant cycle leaves minimal time for the final and most essential step of spending the grant funding. Investments in planning, exercises, and systems development take time and an on-going commitment of stakeholders, in identifying appropriate contractors and in managing the work through to completion. With the 2-year grant cycle and no extensions, we have found ourselves again and again in a position where investments must be prioritized based on their time to completion, rather than their benefit to the region, resulting in a disproportionate investment in equipment. While funding may be spent in a timelier manner, the downstream effect has been a compromise to the overall objectives of the grant.

As a first responder, I see the direct benefit of the Homeland Security grant funding. Being mindful of how each dollar is invested impacts our safety and our ability to protect the public. On April 15, 2013, we were able to utilize not just the equipment, but also the years of planning, exercises, training, and preparedness to maximize life-saving efforts. As the chief, I also oversee our operational budget; I understand the challenges associated with fiscal accountability and the need to work within stringent annual time lines. Ultimately, it is my hope that we can work toward building efficiencies within the grant management process to reduce delays, but also allow the awarding jurisdiction sufficient time to effectively meet the goals of the grant.

Question 2. FEMA has indicated that it would be willing to "reevaluate the feasibility and appropriateness of returning to a 3-year period of performance." Provided we can ensure that an efficient and effective draw-down of these grant funds continues, would you be supportive of a return to a 3-year period of performance?

Answer. I, and the Metro Boston region as a whole, would be in full support of the return to a 3-year period of performance. It would enhance our ability to meet our preparedness goals. Adequately addressing an identified capability gap includes developing a strategy that will incorporate planning, training, and exercising, in addition to equipment.

QUESTIONS FROM CHAIRMAN MICHAEL T. McCAUL FOR BRIAN A. JACKSON [1][2]

APPLYING LESSONS LEARNED FROM PAST RESPONSE OPERATIONS TO STRENGTHENING NATIONAL PREPAREDNESS ADDENDUM

Question 1a. How can we improve the sharing of information developed in a JTTF to outside organizations, such as State and local law enforcement, and fusion centers?

Question 1b. Perhaps some sort of integration between JTTFs and fusion centers?

Question 1c. Do you have any other suggestions as to how we can make the best use of the resources in the fusion centers?

Answer. The sharing of information from JTTFs to other organizations clearly has to be done with care, given concerns regarding maintaining the integrity of criminal investigations and eventual prosecution. This has been a challenge identified for domestic intelligence more generally, not just with respect to the JTTFs.[3] A recent report by three of my RAND colleagues based on discussions with a number of State and local law enforcement officials took on the issue of JTTFs and intelligence sharing directly. Though the group was not a scientific sample of the community, it did represent a set of senior representatives from a number of major departments and

[1] The opinions and conclusions expressed in this testimony are the author's alone and should not be interpreted as representing those of RAND or any of the sponsors of its research. This product is part of the RAND Corporation testimony series. RAND testimonies record testimony presented by RAND associates to Federal, State, or local legislative committees; Government-appointed commissions and panels; and private review and oversight bodies. The RAND Corporation is a non-profit research organization providing objective analysis and effective solutions that address the challenges facing the public and private sectors around the world. RAND's publications do not necessarily reflect the opinions of its research clients and sponsors.

[2] This testimony is available for free download at *http://www.rand.org/pubs/testimonies/CT411z1.html.*

[3] Jackson, BA., ed., "The Challenge of Domestic Intelligence in a Free Society: A Multidisciplinary Look at the Creation of a U.S. Domestic Counterterrorism Intelligence Agency," Santa Monica, Calif., RAND Corporation, 2009.

agencies at varied levels of government.[4] Those participants highlighted continuing challenges with the interaction between JTTFs and local law enforcement, as well as complaints about the nature of the information that was shared. There was also the suggestion of some local departments pulling back from participation in JTTFs because of perceptions of continuing information-sharing problems.

Questions were also raised in those discussions about the effectiveness of information sharing between fusion centers and police departments, though there is clearly variation across the country. The group specifically took on the question of whether fusion centers could be used to better link JTTFs to State and local police departments, and few participants thought that was the right solution. Differences that exist between fusion centers also make it hard to generalize—and the absence of good and objective measures of what they are producing means that there isn't a common yardstick to use to identify, for example, particularly effective fusion centers as candidates to potentially play this bridging role. In the absence of such measures, seeking to use fusion centers in that sort of bridging function could be piloted in one or more sites to assess the viability and effectiveness of the approach.

More systematic measures and assessment of fusion centers would also make it possible to better identify what resources currently exist in individual centers—which are generally viewed to vary considerably in capability across the country—and is a needed first step to determine how they could be better leveraged. Following the 2012 Senate report on the fusion center program,[5] some researchers—including at RAND—have made progress to developing methods for such evaluation.[6]

○

[4] Jenkins, B.M., A. Liepman, H.H. Willis, "Identifying Enemies Among Us: Evolving Terrorist Threats and the Continuing Challenges of Domestic Intelligence Collection and Information Sharing," Santa Monica, Calif., RAND Corporation, 2014.

[5] Permanent Subcommittee on Investigations, Committee on Homeland Security and Governmental Affairs, United States Senate, "Federal Support for and Involvement In State and Local Fusion Centers," Majority and Minority Staff Report, Washington, DC, October 3, 2012.

[6] For example, Jackson, B.A., "How Do We Know What Information Sharing is Really Worth?" Santa Monica, Calif., RAND Corporation, 2014.